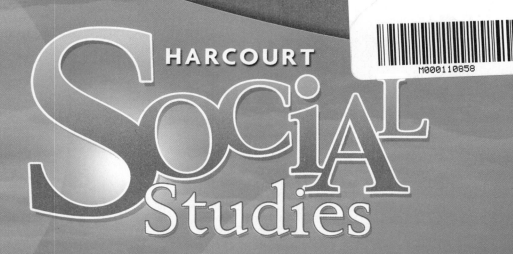

HARCOURT SOCIAL Studies

People Who Make a Difference

Harcourt
SCHOOL PUBLISHERS

HARCOURT SOCIAL Studies

People Who Make a Difference

Series Authors

Dr. Michael J. Berson
Professor
Social Science Education
University of South Florida
Tampa, Florida

Dr. Tyrone C. Howard
Associate Professor
UCLA Graduate School of Education &
   Information Studies
University of California Los Angeles
Los Angeles, California

Dr. Cinthia Salinas
Assistant Professor
Department of Curriculum and Instruction
College of Education
The University of Texas at Austin
Austin, Texas

North Carolina Consultants and Reviewers

Jenny Bajorek
Teacher
Northwoods Elementary School
Cary, North Carolina

Dan Barber
Teacher
Idlewild Elementary School
Charlotte, North Carolina

Brianne Beck
Teacher
Allen Jay Elementary School
High Point, North Carolina

Melissa Blush
Teacher
Allen Jay Elementary School
High Point, North Carolina

Ardelia Brown
Teacher
Pearsontown Elementary School
Durham, North Carolina

Alice M. Cook
Teacher
Paw Creek Elementary School
Charlotte, North Carolina

Lori D. Davis
Teacher
C. Wayne Collier Elementary School
Hope Mills, North Carolina

John D. Ellington
Former Director
Division of Social Studies
North Carolina Department of Public
   Instruction
Raleigh, North Carolina

Laura Griffin
Teacher
Sherwood Park Elementary School
Fayetteville, North Carolina

Sharon Hale
Teacher
Hillandale Elementary School
Durham, North Carolina

Dr. Ted Scott Henson
Educational Consultant
Burlington, North Carolina

Charlotte Heyliger
Teacher
C. Wayne Collier Elementary School
Hope Mills, North Carolina

Tony Iannone
Teacher
Nathaniel Alexander Elementary School
Charlotte, North Carolina

Judith McCray Jones
Educational Consultant
Former Elementary School Administrator
Greensboro, North Carolina

Gwendolyn C. Manning
Teacher
Gibsonville Elementary School
Gibsonville, North Carolina

Courtney McFaull
Teacher
Sherwood Park Elementary School
Fayetteville, North Carolina

Lydia Ogletree O'Rear
Teacher
Elmhurst Elementary School
Greenville, North Carolina

Marsha Rumley
Teacher
Brooks Global Studies
Greensboro, North Carolina

Dean P. Sauls
Teacher
Wayne County Public Schools
Goldsboro, North Carolina

Melissa Turnage
Teacher
Meadow Lane Elementary School
Goldsboro, North Carolina

Joseph E. Webb
Educational Consultant
Adjunct Professor
East Carolina University
Greenville, North Carolina

Harcourt
SCHOOL PUBLISHERS

Copyright © 2009 by Harcourt, Inc.

Printed in the United States of America

ISBN-13: 978-0-15-383133-1
ISBN-10: 0-15-383133-2

6 7 8 9 10   0868   17 16 15 14
4500472917

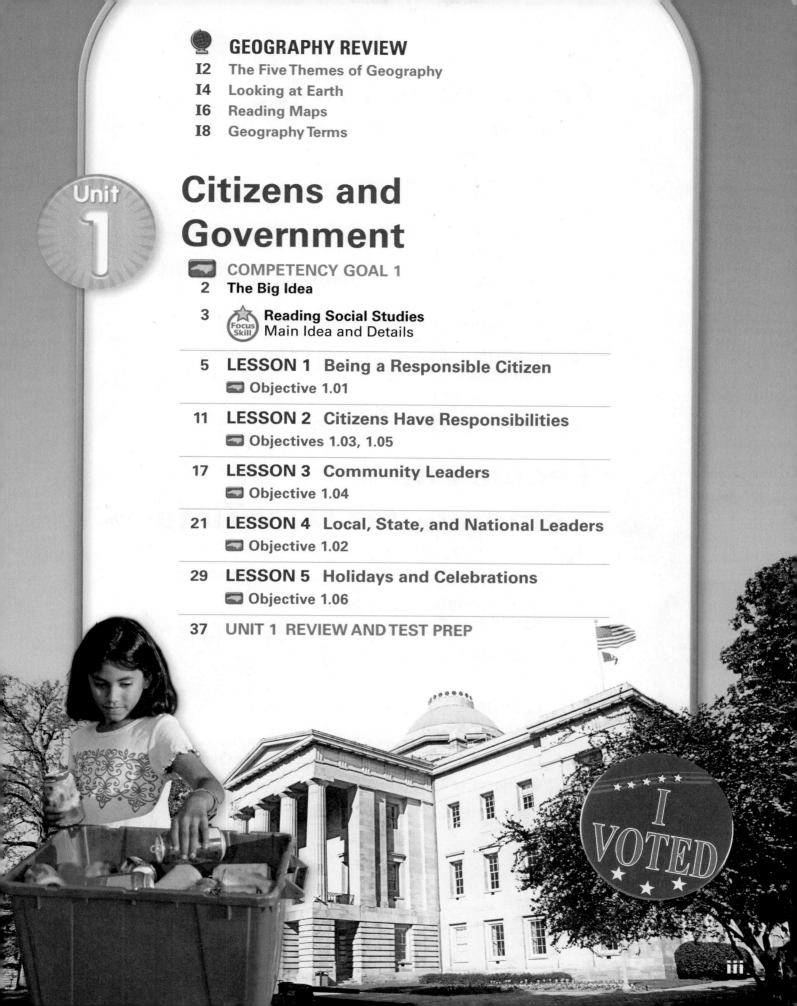

Unit 1

Citizens and Government

Unit 4

Our Geography

COMPETENCY GOAL 4

v

Unit 5

People and Economics

COMPETENCY GOAL 5

Unit

7

People Shape Communities

 COMPETENCY GOAL 7

The Five Themes of Geography

Learning about places is an important part of history and geography. **Geography** is the study of Earth's surface and the ways people use it.

When geographers study Earth, they often think about five main themes, or topics. Keep these themes in mind as you read. They will help you think like a geographer.

Geography

Location

Everything on Earth has its own **location** — the place where it can be found.

Place

Every place has physical and human characteristics, or features, that make it different from all other places. **Physical features** are formed by nature. **Human features** are created by people.

Human-Environment Interactions

The environment may affect people, causing them to **adapt**, or adjust, to their surroundings.

Movement

Each day, people in different parts of our country and around the world exchange products and ideas.

Themes

Regions

Areas of Earth that share features that make them different from other areas are called **regions**. A region can be described by its physical features or its human features.

Looking at Earth

A distant view from space shows Earth's round shape. The shape of Earth is shown best by a globe. A **globe** is a model of our planet.

Like Earth, a globe is a sphere, or ball. A globe shows Earth's major bodies of water and its continents. **Continents** are the largest land masses. Because of its shape, a globe can only show one half of Earth at a time. On a map of the world, you can see all of the land and water at once.

The World

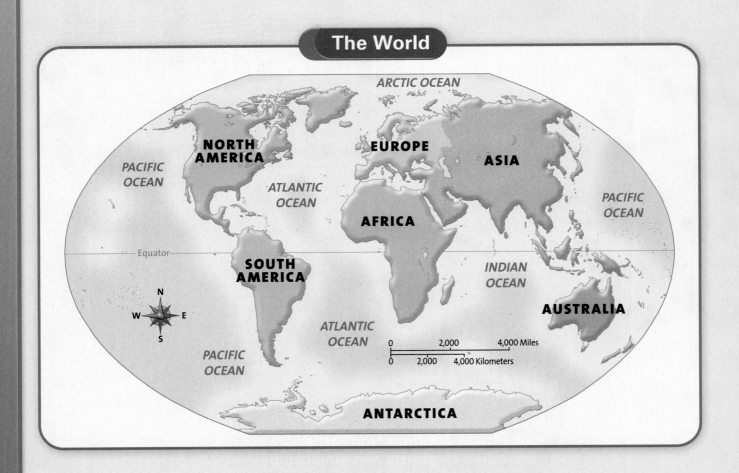

Halfway between the North Pole and South Pole is an imaginary line called the **equator**. It divides Earth into two equal halves, or **hemispheres**. The Northern Hemisphere is north of the equator. The Southern Hemisphere is south of it.

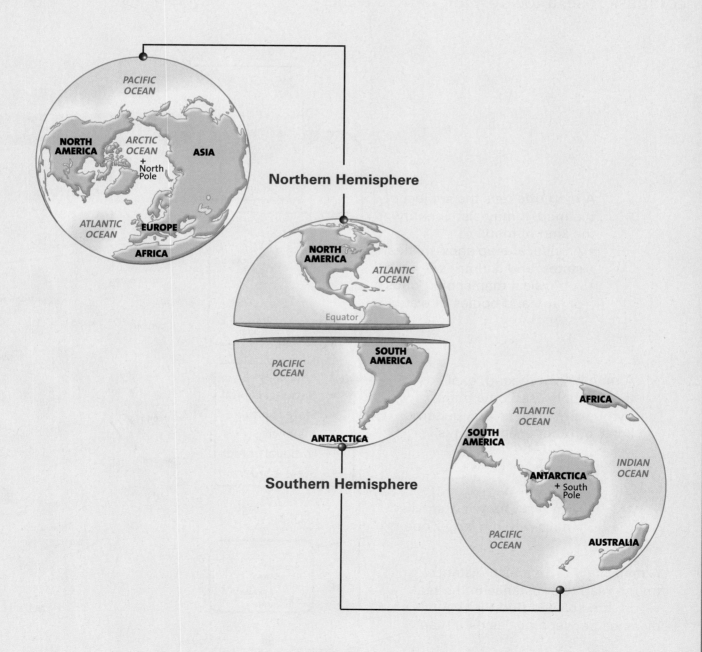

Northern Hemisphere

Southern Hemisphere

Reading Maps

Maps can provide you with many kinds of information about Earth and the world around you. To help you read maps more easily, mapmakers add certain features to most maps they draw. These features usually include a map title, a map key, a compass rose, a locator, and a map scale.

A **locator** is a small map or globe that shows where the place on the main map is located within a larger area.

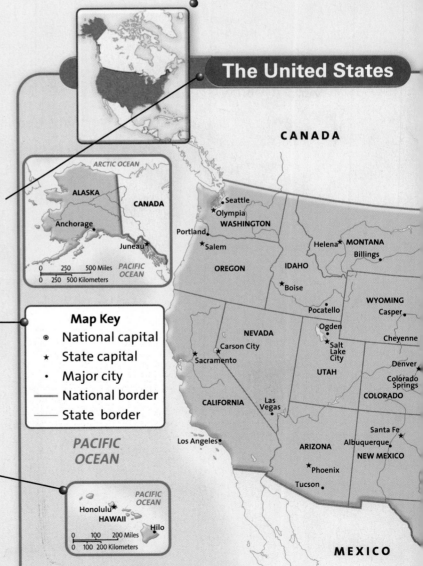

The United States

A **map title** tells the subject of the map. It may also identify the kind of map.
- A political map shows cities, states, and countries.
- A physical map shows kinds of land and bodies of water.

A **map key**, or legend, explains the symbols used on a map. Symbols may be colors, patterns, lines, or other special marks.

An **inset map** is a smaller map within a larger one.

A **map scale** compares a distance on the map to a distance in the real world. It helps you find the real distance between places on a map.

Map Key
- ⊛ National capital
- ★ State capital
- · Major city
- — National border
- — State border

Mapmakers sometimes need to show places marked on a map in greater detail or places that are located beyond the area shown on the map. Find Alaska and Hawaii on the map below. To show this much detail for these states and the rest of the country, the map would have to be much larger. Instead, Alaska and Hawaii are shown in separate inset maps, or a small map within a larger map.

A **compass rose**, or direction marker, shows directions.
• The **cardinal directions** are north, south, east, and west.
• The **intermediate directions**, or directions between the cardinal directions, are northeast, northwest, southeast, and southwest.

Geography Terms

① **desert** a large, dry area of land

② **forest** a large area of trees

③ **gulf** a large body of ocean water that is partly surrounded by land

④ **hill** land that rises above the land around it

⑤ **island** a landform with water all around it

⑥ **lake** a body of water with land on all sides

⑦ **mountain** the highest kind of land

⑧ **ocean** a body of salt water that covers a large area

⑨ **peninsula** a landform that is surrounded on only three sides by water

⑩ **plain** flat land

⑪ **river** a large stream of water that flows across the land

⑫ **valley** low land between hills or mountains

Citizens and Government

Spotlight on Goals and Objectives

North Carolina Interactive Presentations

NORTH CAROLINA STANDARD COURSE OF STUDY

COMPETENCY GOAL 1 The learner will characterize qualities of good citizenship by identifying people who made a difference in the community and other social environments.

State Capitol building, Raleigh, North Carolina

⚲ The Big Idea

How do people work together to make a difference in their community and in the communities of others?

People in a community help each other every day. They work together to make their community a better place to live. People may help at schools or help clean up litter. They also work together to care for the people living in their community. Some people hold food drives or donate clothing. Others work to make communities better places to live. By working together to care for the people and the community, people can make a difference.

Describe one way people work together in your community to make it a better place to live.

Who are the people? _____

_____

_____

What do they do? _____

_____

_____

Why do they do it? _____

_____

_____

Main Idea and Details

▶ Learn

- The **main idea** is the most important idea of a paragraph. It is often in the first sentence of a paragraph.
- **Details** give more information about the main idea.

Main Idea

The most important idea

Details

Facts about the main idea	Facts about the main idea	Facts about the main idea

▶ Practice

Read the paragraph. Circle the main idea. Then underline two details.

Many people in North Carolina work to make a difference in their community. Some people join groups that work to help people. One group that people join is the North Carolina Commission on Volunteerism and Community Service.

Main Idea

Detail

Read the following paragraphs.

Making a Difference in North Carolina

The North Carolina Commission on Volunteerism and Community Service was set up in 1993. It provides opportunities for people to help make a difference in their community.

People can work with the North Carolina Commission on Volunteerism and Community Service in many ways. Some people help clean up their community. Others build houses for people who need them. Some teach people to speak English.

The commission works with people of all ages. One part of the commission is a group of students called Learn and Serve. Students who work with this group can learn about government and the environment while serving their community.

Add the details that support the main idea in the chart below.

Main Idea

The North Carolina Commission on Volunteerism and Community Service helps people in North Carolina make a difference in their community.

Details

Being a Responsible Citizen

Citizens have a responsibility to show respect for others and for themselves. Responsible citizens around the world give their time, money, and skills to help make their communities better places to live. **What will you learn about being a responsible citizen?**

_____

_____

**NORTH CAROLINA
STANDARD COURSE OF STUDY**

1.01 Identify and demonstrate characteristics of responsible citizenship and explain how citizen participation can impact changes within a community.

TextWork

1 Underline the definition of the term *common good*.

2 Circle two examples of work people do for the common good.

Citizens Make a Difference

Every community has people who work for the **common good**, or the good of everyone. Some help build homes for their neighbors. Others work to help the environment. While their work may be different, these people all work to improve their communities.

Many citizens help their communities by working as volunteers. A **volunteer** is a person who chooses to work without pay. Volunteers help their communities in many ways. In times of trouble, such as after a hurricane, volunteers may collect food, clothing, and medicine for people who need them.

❯ Volunteers help people after a tsunami in Asia (inset) and after Hurricane Katrina (below).

▶ **Habitat for Humanity volunteers work in communities across the United States.**

Boone, North Carolina

Helping others is one way to work for the common good. In Boone, North Carolina, many people volunteer for Habitat for Humanity. This group builds houses for people who cannot afford the full cost of a house. Since 1987, Habitat for Humanity volunteers have built more than 17 houses in Watauga County, North Carolina.

Some volunteers work in Boone's Habitat ReStore. This store sells used building materials. Money made from the Habitat ReStore goes toward the cost of building new houses. It also helps the community reduce waste because parts of old houses are not thrown away.

 **TextWork**

❸ Circle examples of volunteers in the pictures on pages 6–7.

❹ Underline two ways in which the Habitat ReStore helps the community.

TextWork

5 Who raised money to help Joel Gomez?

_____

_____

Wheaton, Illinois

People in the community of Wheaton, Illinois, helped one of its citizens. Joel Gomez was hurt while fighting in the war in Iraq. He could no longer move his body and had to use a wheelchair.

Volunteers from more than 50 groups in Wheaton helped Joel Gomez. One group of volunteers worked to build him a new house. School groups and firefighters held events to raise money for Gomez. One citizen even bought him a van.

❯ **Volunteers helped build a house (below) for Joel Gomez (inset) in Wheaton, Illinois.**

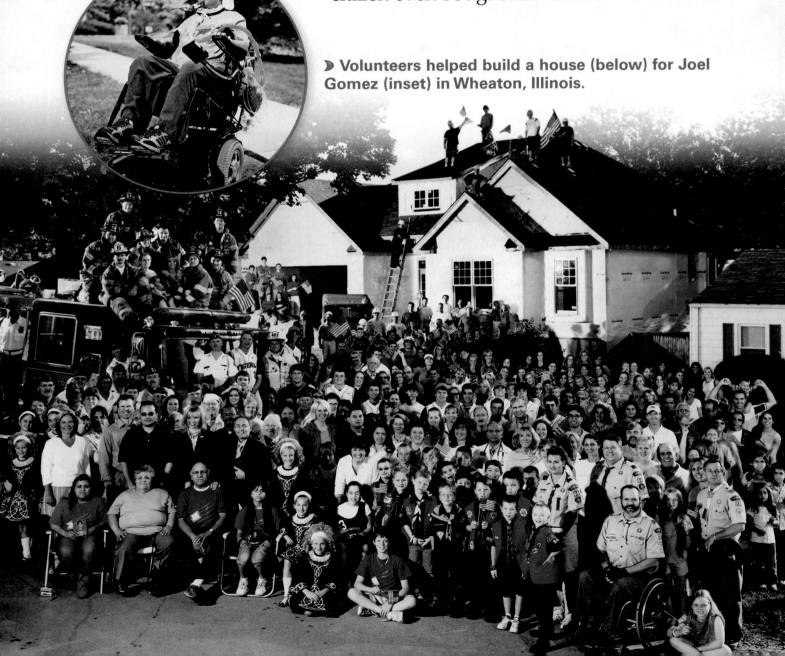

▶ People care for the environment by recycling
and setting aside areas of land.

Caring for the Environment

Responsible citizens can help take care of the environment. By protecting land and water, people can make their communities better. One way to do this is to set aside areas of land and water for protection. For example, the Cape Hatteras National Seashore protects 70 miles of the Outer Banks of North Carolina.

People also help protect the environment when they **recycle**, or reuse, products. Newspapers, cardboard, and many kinds of plastic can be recycled. Glass from jars and bottles and aluminum from cans can be reused. By recycling, people reduce the amount of trash that is thrown away.

 TextWork

6 What does the word *recycle* mean?

_____

7 Circle five examples of products and materials that people recycle.

1. **SUMMARIZE** How can you be a responsible citizen?

_____

_____

_____

_____

_____

2. How can a **volunteer** help his or her community?

_____

_____

_____

3. How can people help protect the environment?

_____

_____

_____

4. What are some ways in which you can help to make your community a better place to live?

_____

_____

_____

_____

Circle the letter of the correct answer.

5. What is a responsible citizen?

   A a person who cares about others and works for the common good

   B a person who lives in a community

   C a person who litters

   D a person who pollutes the environment

writing

✏ **Write a Paragraph** Write a paragraph that describes how citizens can help make their communities better places.

Citizens Have Responsibilities

Firefighters teach students about fire safety

United States citizens have many civic responsibilities. They must act responsibly to keep their towns and cities safe. They also have the civic responsibility to follow laws and to vote. Citizens have the responsibilities of paying taxes and serving on juries, too. **What will you learn about civic responsibilities?**

_____

_____

NORTH CAROLINA STANDARD COURSE OF STUDY

1.03 Identify and explain the importance of civic responsibility, including but not limited to, obeying laws and voting.

1.05 Suggest responsible courses of action in given situations and assess the consequences of irresponsible behavior.

 **TextWork**

① Why do communities have governments?

_____

_____

_____

② Circle in the text two examples of traffic laws.

Rules and Laws

Communities have governments to make rules and laws. A **government** is a group of people that makes laws for a community, a state, or a country. The government makes laws about how citizens should behave and makes sure laws are obeyed.

Laws help people know what to do and what not to do. Laws keep order in a community. Laws help keep people safe. For example, traffic laws help people travel safely. Speed limits protect people on the streets and highways. Laws about wearing seat belts protect people in cars.

▶ A crossing guard helps students and drivers obey the law.

It is important for people to understand and obey the laws of their community. When people obey the laws, they keep their community safe and peaceful.

People who break laws must face consequences (KAHN•suh•kwen•suhz). A **consequence** is what happens as a result of what a person does. If someone breaks a law, one consequence may be having to pay an amount of money as punishment. The consequence for breaking some laws may be as serious as going to jail.

TextWork

❸ What might be one consequence of breaking a law?

_____

_____

_____

❹ Circle the pictures that show people who make sure laws are being followed in a community.

BUCKLE UP IT'S THE LAW

People must register, or sign up, to vote (inset). Voters use booths that keep their choices secret (above).

TextWork

5 How old must a citizen be to vote?

_____

6 Circle the person in the pictures above who is registering to vote.

Citizens Make Choices

Voting is an important civic responsibility. By voting, citizens can choose their government leaders. Citizens must be at least 18 years old to vote. They must follow the voting rules in their state.

An **election** is a time set aside for voting. On the day of an election, voters mark their choices on a ballot on paper or on a voting machine. A **ballot** lists all of the choices or candidates in an election. A **candidate** is a person who wants to be elected as a leader. Citizens should learn about the candidates before voting.

Each citizen's vote in an election is kept secret. People can vote without worrying about what others may think of their choices. Only the final results are announced.

Paying Taxes and Serving on Juries

Citizens also have a civic responsibility to pay taxes. There are city, county, state, and national taxes. Taxes give the government money to pay for the services people need. Governments use tax money to build roads, parks, and schools. Taxes also pay for workers, such as teachers, firefighters, and police officers.

Serving on a jury is a civic responsibility. A **jury** is a group of citizens who sit in a courtroom and listen to the facts of a case. A jury decides whether a person has broken a law. If a jury decides that a person is guilty, the judge decides his or her punishment. Juries are an important part of our government.

TextWork

7 Why do people pay taxes?

_____

_____

_____

8 Look at the picture below. Circle the people who are serving on a jury.

> A jury has a responsibility to make careful decisions.

1. **SUMMARIZE** Why is it important for people to meet their civic responsibilities?

_____

_____

_____

_____

2. Use **consequence** in a sentence about rules and laws.

_____

_____

_____

3. How do citizens choose their leaders?

_____

_____

4. How does a government use money collected as taxes?

_____

_____

_____

_____

5. What responsibilities do voters have?

_____

_____

_____

writing

✎ **Write a Speech** Write a speech that tells about the civic responsibilities of citizens.

Community Leaders

Lesson 3

Every community needs leaders. Leaders make life better for citizens by doing work for the good of the community. Some leaders are a part of the government. Others work by themselves or with a group to help their community. **What will you learn about community leaders?**

_____

_____

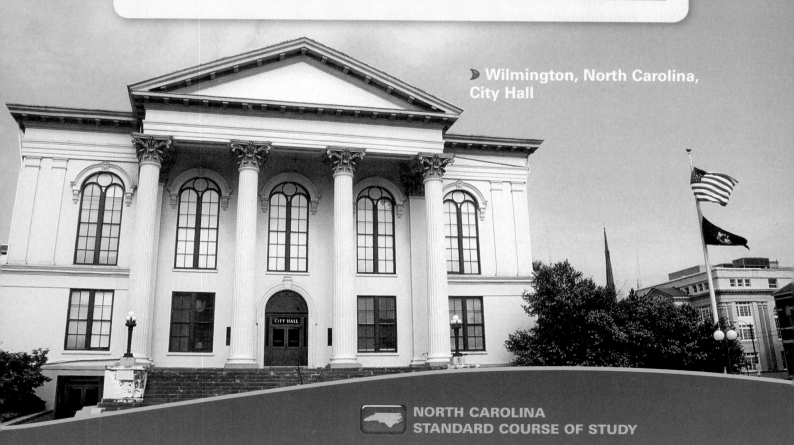

◗ **Wilmington, North Carolina, City Hall**

CITY HALL

NORTH CAROLINA STANDARD COURSE OF STUDY

1.04 Explain the need for leaders in communities and describe their roles and responsibilities.

▶ The mayor of Charlotte works at Charlotte City Hall (above).

❶ How do citizens elect public servants?

_____

_____

❷ Underline two examples of elected leaders.

Elected Leaders

Some leaders are a part of the government. Community leaders who work in the government are called public servants. A **public servant** is someone who makes decisions and takes action for the community. Citizens often vote to elect public servants. Elected leaders might include mayors, judges, and members of the city council, town council, or county government. These government leaders meet to talk about and make decisions about community problems.

Appointed and Civic Leaders

Some leaders are not elected. They are chosen by elected government leaders to do jobs, such as running the police and fire departments. Government leaders **appoint**, or name, people to do these jobs.

Civic leaders also work for the good of their community. These leaders may include elected leaders such as mayors. However, many civic leaders are not elected or appointed. Civic leaders can work alone or with a group. Members of a Parent-Teacher Association work to improve schools in their community. Members of a neighborhood association help make their community clean and safe.

TextWork

❸ List two examples of appointed leaders.

_____

_____

_____

❹ What type of leader was Cesar Chavez?

_____

_____

Biography

Fairness

Cesar Chavez

Cesar Chavez was a civic leader. He spent his life working to make sure people were treated fairly. In 1962, he formed a union known today as the United Farm Workers of America. The union held strikes to get farmworkers better pay and better working conditions. In a strike, people will not work until they are treated fairly.

Time

1927	1993
Born	Died

1962 Starts union known today as the United Farm Workers of America

1. **SUMMARIZE** Why do communities need leaders?

_____

_____

_____

_____

_____

2. List two examples of community leaders who are **public servants**.

_____

_____

_____

3. How are elected leaders different from appointed leaders?

_____

_____

_____

_____

4. How do civic leaders help a community?

_____

_____

_____

5. How did Cesar Chavez help farmworkers?

_____

_____

_____

activity

Make a Bulletin Board Make a bulletin board about the leaders in your community.

Local, State, and National Leaders

Senator Richard Burr with his wife, Brooke, and Vice President Dick Cheney

Local, state, and national leaders work to solve problems in North Carolina. These leaders work to keep citizens of the state safe. They also help make laws and help provide government services that people need. A **government service** is work that the government does for everyone in a community. **What will you learn about local, state, and national leaders?**

_____

_____

**NORTH CAROLINA
STANDARD COURSE OF STUDY**

1.02 Recognize diverse local, state, and national leaders, past and present, who demonstrate responsible citizenship.

❶ Circle the three main levels of government in the illustration below.

❷ Underline the text that describes how Howard Lee demonstrated responsible citizenship.

❸ Circle two ways that Milton Hunt has helped the community of Pembroke.

Local Leaders

Our country has three main levels of government—local, state, and national. Leaders at each level of government have many responsibilities in common. However, these leaders have separate responsibilities.

Local Government

North Carolina has two types of local government—city and county. People who live in the cities and counties elect their local leaders. These leaders offer government services for their communities. Local governments build and keep up local roads, schools, and parks. They provide services, such as fighting fires, enforcing laws, and collecting trash.

Levels of Government

❯ This illustration shows the different levels of government.

Raleigh

Local

Howard Lee

In 1969, Howard Lee was elected mayor of Chapel Hill, North Carolina. Lee served three terms as mayor. He demonstrated responsible citizenship by setting up a program to help families borrow money to buy and improve homes. He is also the chairman of the North Carolina State Board of Education.

Milton Hunt

Milton Hunt is the mayor of Pembroke, North Carolina. Pembroke is an American Indian community. Most of the people who live there are members of the Lumbee tribe. Hunt has been mayor of Pembroke for more than 20 years. He has helped it grow by bringing businesses to the area. He has also worked to gain rights for the Lumbee tribe.

> Howard Lee

> Milton Hunt

North Carolina

The United States

State

National

State Leaders

State leaders are often elected into state governments. State governments take care of state parks and state highways. Each state provides driver's licenses and public education for citizens. Not all state leaders are in government. Some work with groups that serve the state's communities.

James Holshouser

In 1973, James Holshouser was elected governor of North Carolina. A **governor** is the elected leader of the state government. As governor, Holshouser focused on improving North Carolina's schools and state parks. He also set up health clinics for people who lived far away from doctors' offices and hospitals.

❯ The Executive Mansion in Raleigh, North Carolina, was completed in 1891. It is the home of the state's governor.

❯ James Holshouser, former governor of North Carolina

❯ Mike Easley, current governor of North Carolina

▶ M. Zulayka Santiago, Executive Director of El Pueblo, Inc.

M. Zulayka Santiago

M. Zulayka Santiago is the Executive Director of El Pueblo, Inc. It is located in Raleigh, North Carolina. This group helps the Hispanic American community in North Carolina. It teaches people in the community about Hispanic people, culture, and history. Santiago also works with other state leaders to make sure that all students in North Carolina get a good education.

TextWork

❹ Who is the current governor of North Carolina?

_____

❺ Underline two examples of work that James Holshouser did to improve North Carolina.

❻ Circle one example of work that M. Zulayka Santiago does that helps students in North Carolina.

National Leaders

The national government protects our country. It works with the governments of other countries, too. Each of the 50 states elects two senators to serve as representatives in the national government. A **representative** is a person chosen by a group of people to act or speak for them.

Sam Ervin

Sam Ervin served as a United States senator from North Carolina for 20 years. Ervin was considered an expert on the United States Constitution. He worked hard to uphold its teachings. Before he served in the United States Senate, he served in the state assembly and on the state supreme court.

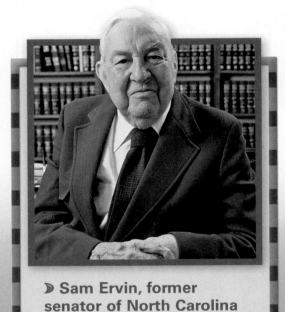

▶ Sam Ervin, former senator of North Carolina

▶ The United States Senate meets in the Capitol building in Washington, D.C.

Elizabeth Dole

As a community leader, Elizabeth Dole has always tried to act responsibly. In 2002, she became the first woman elected from North Carolina to the United States Senate. As a senator, Dole has worked to make workplaces safer and to make working conditions fair. She also works to improve the education, health, and safety of the people of North Carolina.

TextWork

❾ List three examples of work Elizabeth Dole does for the people of North Carolina.

_____

_____

_____

▶ Senator Elizabeth Dole

1. **SUMMARIZE** How do local, state, and national leaders demonstrate responsible citizenship?

_____

_____

_____

_____

_____

_____

2. What is a **representative**?

_____

_____

_____

_____

_____

3. What kinds of services do local governments provide?

_____

_____

_____

4. What are two responsibilities of a state government?

_____

_____

_____

Circle the letter of the correct answer.

5. Who is the elected leader of the state government?

   A senator

   B mayor

   C governor

   D director

writing

✎ **Do Research** Use the library or the Internet to find out who represents your community in the national government. Write a paragraph that describes what these people have done for your community.

Holidays and Celebrations

People often celebrate American history on national holidays. A **holiday** is a day set aside for remembering a person, an idea, or an event. People also celebrate their **culture**, or ways of life, on special days. **What will you learn about the holidays that people celebrate?**

_____

_____

▷ The Grandfather Mountain Highland Games in Linville, North Carolina

**NORTH CAROLINA
STANDARD COURSE OF STUDY**

1.06 Identify selected personalities associated with major holidays and cultural celebrations.

▶ People in the United States celebrate our country's freedom and the Declaration of Independence (inset) on the Fourth of July.

Celebrating Events

National holidays celebrate important events in our country's history.

Independence Day

On July 4, 1776, our country's leaders voted to accept the Declaration of Independence. It was written by some of our country's early leaders. John Adams, Benjamin Franklin, and Thomas Jefferson all helped write the Declaration of Independence.

Every year on the Fourth of July, we celebrate Independence Day. On this day, we remember the people who fought for our country's independence, or freedom. Many people across the country gather to watch fireworks displays. Others fly the American flag. Some people show pride in the United States by wearing red, white, and blue.

TextWork

❶ What do national holidays celebrate?

_____

_____

❷ Circle the names of the authors of the Declaration of Independence.

❸ On what day do we celebrate our country's independence?

_____

Constitution Day

On September 17, 1787, the leaders of the United States signed the Constitution. A **constitution** is a written set of laws that tells how a government will work. Congress passed a law in 2004, making September 17 Constitution Day. On this day, people celebrate the Constitution and honor the leaders who wrote it.

Thanksgiving

Thanksgiving is a national holiday in late November. It celebrates harvesttime and other reasons to be thankful. On this day, Americans remember a feast. This feast was shared by the Pilgrims of Plymouth, Massachusetts, and the Wampanoag Indians. It celebrated the Pilgrims' first harvest in 1621.

❯ People celebrate Constitution Day by reciting the Pledge of Allegiance (inset). The Pilgrims share their harvest with the Wampanoag Indians (below).

TextWork

4 Why do people celebrate Constitution Day?

_____

_____

5 When was the first Thanksgiving celebrated?

_____

▶ On Dr. Martin Luther King, Jr., Day, people remember King and the changes that he helped bring about.

▶ George Washington was the first President of the United States.

Celebrating People

Some national holidays celebrate people.

Dr. Martin Luther King, Jr., Day

In January, people celebrate the birthday of African American leader Dr. Martin Luther King, Jr. King spoke out against unfair laws and stood up for civil rights for all people. **Civil rights** are rights that give everyone equal treatment. Today, Dr. Martin Luther King, Jr., Day honors Dr. King and his peaceful actions for civil rights.

Presidents' Day

In February, we celebrate Presidents' Day. This holiday once marked the birthday of George Washington. Now it honors all United States Presidents.

Memorial Day and Veterans Day

In May, our country celebrates Memorial Day. On this day, people remember the citizens who have given their lives for our country.

In November, we celebrate Veterans Day. On this day, we honor all of the citizens who have served in our country's military.

Columbus Day

Columbus Day honors the Italian explorer Christopher Columbus and his voyage to the Americas. It is celebrated on the second Monday of October. On Columbus Day, many American cities have parades.

TextWork

❻ Underline the text that explains what is honored on Dr. Martin Luther King, Jr., Day.

❼ Why do people in the United States celebrate Presidents' Day?

_____

_____

❽ Which holiday honors people who have served in the military?

_____

▶ People who are dressed as soldiers from the American Revolution take part in a Veterans Day parade.

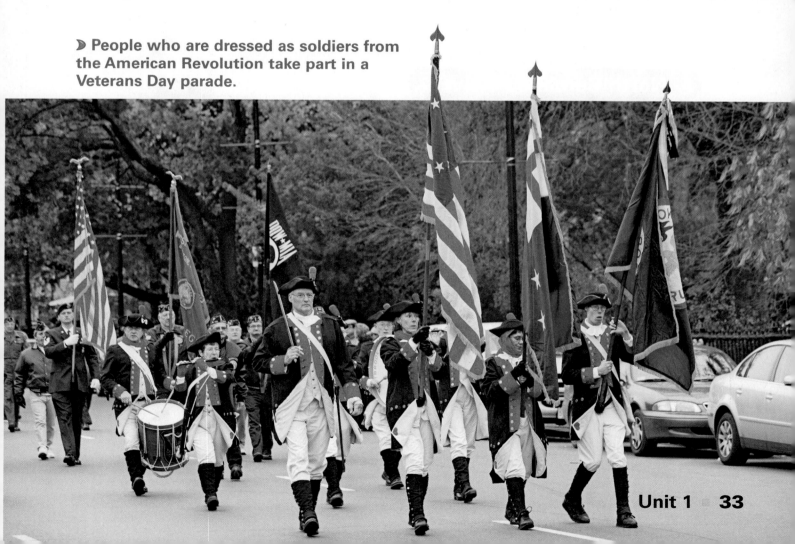

TextWork

9 Underline the text that describes Celebrate Our State: A North Carolina Festival.

10 Circle the picture that shows an American Indian celebration.

Celebrating Cultures

Cultural celebrations can help people learn about different cultures. Many celebrations in North Carolina honor cultures found in the state, in surrounding states, and around the world.

North Carolina Cultural Festivals

Celebrate Our State: A North Carolina Festival celebrates the music and culture of North Carolina. It is held each year in High Point, North Carolina. At this festival, visitors enjoy Appalachian folk, bluegrass, and beach music.

North Carolina Festivals

Mountain Song Festival in Brevard, North Carolina

American Indian Pow Wow in Charlotte, North Carolina

There are other festivals that celebrate the state's musical heritage, too. The Mountain Dance and Folk Festival takes place in Asheville. The Bluegrass and Old Time Fiddler's Convention takes place in Mount Airy.

Folkmoot USA

Since 1984, Folkmoot USA has celebrated the cultures of countries around the world. This international folk festival hosts many performances throughout Haywood County in western North Carolina. Musicians and dancers from countries such as Germany, the Netherlands, Ireland, Turkey, Mexico, and India perform at Folkmoot USA.

TextWork

⓫ In what year did Folkmoot USA begin?

_____

⓬ Circle the names of countries that take part in Folkmoot USA.

Mexican dancers perform at Folkmoot USA in North Carolina

Yiasou Greek Festival in Charlotte, North Carolina

1. **SUMMARIZE** Why are cultural celebrations and holidays important?

_____

_____

_____

_____

2. Write a sentence about the importance of **civil rights**.

_____

_____

3. How does your community celebrate national holidays?

_____

_____

_____

4. How can national holidays help us think about our country's heritage?

_____

_____

_____

_____

MATCHING Draw a line connecting each person or group on the left with the related holiday on the right.

5. Benjamin Franklin   Thanksgiving

6. Wampanoag Indians   Memorial Day

7. People who gave their
   lives for our country   Independence Day

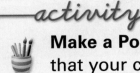

activity

Make a Poster Make a poster about a holiday that your community celebrates.

Review and Test Prep

Unit 1

The Big Idea

People work together to make a difference in their community and in the communities of others.

Summarize the Unit

Main Idea and Details Complete the graphic organizer to show that you understand the important idea and details about the ways people make a difference in communities.

Main Idea

People make a difference in communities.

Details

Use Vocabulary

Draw a line connecting each term with its definition.

1. a time set aside for voting   **volunteer,** p. 6

2. someone who makes decisions and takes action for the community   **election,** p. 14

3. a person who works without pay   **public servant,** p. 18

4. a day set aside for remembering a person or an event   **holiday,** p. 29

Think About It

5. List two ways in which people can care for the environment.

_____

_____

6. Why do citizens pay taxes?

_____

_____

7. What is the role of government leaders?

_____

_____

Circle the letter of the correct answer.

8. Which is a leader who serves in the state government?

   A a mayor

   B a governor

   C a senator

   D a candidate

9. What is culture?

   A ways of life

   B a festival

   C a map

   D a lake

Show What You Know

Writing Write a Summary
Describe the relationship between citizens and their government.

Activity Create a Bulletin Board
Draw or cut out pictures of people who have made a difference in your community. Write captions that explain who the people are and why you chose them.

GO online To play a game that reviews the unit, join Eco in the North Carolina Adventures online or on CD.

Our Different Roles

Spotlight on Goals and Objectives

North Carolina Interactive Presentations

NORTH CAROLINA STANDARD COURSE OF STUDY

COMPETENCY GOAL 2 The learner will analyze the multiple roles that individuals perform in families, workplaces, and communities.

▶ At school, the role of children is to be students.

The Big Idea

What roles do people have in families, at work, and in communities?

      People have different roles, or parts they play, in families, at work, and in communities. They work together to help solve problems, keep each other safe, and provide things they want and need. At home, your role might be to help around the house. Other members in your family count on you to help. Your role at school is to be a student. Your teacher counts on you to listen and learn. You also have a role in your community. It is to be a good citizen. Others in your community count on you to make good choices. The ways in which people count on one another may be different. However, all people in families, at work, and in communities can share with and learn from one another.

Think of a person in your community and the role this person has. Then answer the questions below.

Who is the person? _____

What does this person do in your community? _____

_____

Who counts on this person? _____

_____

What would happen if this person did not do what he

or she is supposed to do? _____

_____

Reading Social Studies

 Summarize

▶ Learn

- When you **summarize**, you retell the main idea and the most important details of a passage.
- You can often summarize a paragraph or even a whole selection in just one sentence.

Key Facts		Summary
Important fact from the reading	⮕	Important information, shortened and written in your own words
Important fact from the reading	⮕	

▶ Practice

Read the paragraph. Then summarize it in one sentence.

Charles M. Duke, Jr., was born in Charlotte in 1935. **Key Fact**
In 1966, Duke became the first astronaut from North
Carolina. He was one of 19 people chosen at that time
to be an astronaut.

_____

_____

➤ Apply

Read the following paragraphs.

Charles M. Duke, Jr.

Charles M. Duke, Jr., graduated from the Air Force Aerospace Research Pilot School in 1965. He stayed at the school to teach people how to fly airplanes and jets. The training he got there would later help him as an astronaut.

In April 1972, Duke took part in the *Apollo 16* mission. During that mission, he spent more than 71 hours on the moon's surface. He is one of only 12 people ever to walk on the moon.

In 1975, Duke retired from the astronaut program and started his own business. Duke is a husband, a father, and a grandfather. He has two sons and five grandchildren.

Use the key facts below to summarize the selection about Charles M. Duke, Jr.

Key Fact

Duke graduated from the Air Force Aerospace Research Pilot School in 1965.

Key Fact

In 1975, Duke retired from the astronaut program and started his own business.

Summary

_____

_____

_____

_____

_____

_____

_____

Our Roles in the Community

Children and adults have roles in their communities. A **role** is the part a person plays in a community or a group. Children and adults have different roles at work, at home, and at school. Their roles may also be different depending on where they live. **What might you learn about our different roles?**

_____

_____

**NORTH CAROLINA
STANDARD COURSE OF STUDY**

2.01 Distinguish and compare economic and social roles of children and adults in the local community to selected communities around the world.

❶ Underline the definition of the word *economy*.

❷ Circle four ways in which children can earn money.

❸ What are two things children may do with their money as part of their economic roles?

_____

_____

_____

_____

▶ **Children may save money (below) that they earn by doing chores (top right).**

Our Economic Roles

An **economy** is the way the people of a country or a community make and use goods and services. A **good** is something that can be bought and sold. A **service** is work that a person does for someone else. How people earn and use money is part of their economic roles.

Economic Roles of Children

Many children do chores at home to earn money. Other children do jobs, such as walking dogs or doing yard work, for people in the community. In places around the world, some children work on family farms and in family businesses. Children may save their money. Children may also use their money to buy things they want or to help others.

Economic Roles of Adults

Adults do many kinds of jobs to earn money. Some adults may earn money by growing, making, or selling goods. In North Carolina, some people grow crops. Others may work in factories that make goods such as furniture, cloth, or computers. Some adults offer services. They may work in hotels, at theme parks, or in museums.

In communities around the world, adults work to earn money. Some adults work on farms or sell food in markets. Other adults make goods, such as blankets or pottery. They sell these goods in markets or trade them for other goods.

Adults use the money they earn in many ways. They may buy the things they want and need. They may save money in banks. They may also choose to share their money to help others in the community.

TextWork

❹ Circle two ways in which adults can earn money.

❺ Circle the picture that shows an adult using money he or she has earned.

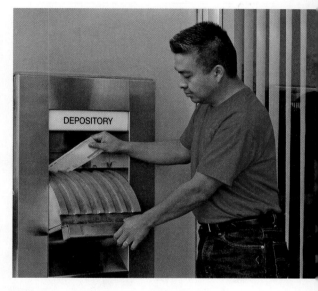

▶ A man deposits money at a bank.

▶ A woman sells crafts at a market in Ecuador.

Our Social Roles

A **society** is a community of people joined together by similar ways of life. Both children and adults have social roles in society.

Social Roles of Children

Children have social roles in their families. They may be brothers or sisters. They may also be grandchildren.

Children also have social roles in their communities. A child's main social role is to be a student. School helps prepare children for their roles as adults.

At most schools in Japan, students study math, science, social studies, and English. They also study arts that are important to their culture, such as origami.

❯ Japanese students study origami, or the art of paper folding (inset), and many other subjects at school (below).

> A police officer helps keep a community safe (left). At school, students learn to work together (inset).

Children around the world also have social roles in different groups. Some children play team sports, such as soccer. Others join groups, such as Scouts, to learn skills or to help the community.

Social Roles of Adults

Adults also have social roles. They may be parents, aunts or uncles, or grand-parents. Being a friend or a neighbor is another adult social role. Some adults also volunteer to work in groups that help other people.

Some social roles can be economic roles, too. For example, helping keep people in the community safe is a police officer's social role. Earning money by working is the police officer's economic role.

TextWork

9 List two examples of social roles of children in groups.

_____

_____

10 Underline three examples of social roles of adults.

11 Look at the pictures above. Circle the person who has an economic role and a social role at the same time.

1. **SUMMARIZE** What kinds of economic roles and social roles do people have in communities?

_____

_____

_____

2. What is an **economy**?

_____

_____

_____

3. How are the economic roles of people in all communities similar?

_____

_____

_____

_____

4. How are the social roles of people in all communities similar?

_____

_____

_____

_____

_____

5. Which is a child's main social role?

   A grandparent

   B police officer

   C student

   D parent

activity

Make a Chart Make a chart that shows the economic and social roles in your family and in your community. Compare your roles with the economic and social roles of your parents.

Families in Different Times and Places

Since **ancient** times, or times very long ago, families have lived and worked together in communities. In some ways, families have stayed the same over time. In other ways, families have changed over time. **What will you learn about families living long ago?**

now they cooked

Today, visitors to Plimoth Plantation in Massachusetts can see what life was like in the 1600s.

**NORTH CAROLINA
STANDARD COURSE OF STUDY**

2.02 Analyze similarities and differences among families in different times and in different places.

❶ Underline the name of an early community that began in Mesopotamia.

❷ List one way in which the roles of boys in ancient Sumer were different from the roles of girls.

① Sumer

② boys

▶ This clay tablet shows Sumerian writing.

Ancient Mesopotamia

One of the world's earliest communities was Sumer. It was in southwestern Asia in a place called Mesopotamia. In Sumer, men worked outside of the home as merchants and craftworkers. Women took care of the home. Boys from wealthy families studied reading, writing, and math. Other boys learned how to do their fathers' jobs. Girls helped their mothers with jobs at home, such as cooking and weaving.

Ancient Greece

Athens was an important community in ancient Greece. All free men over the age of 18 could take part in government.

Women who were wealthy ran large homes, overseeing servants and slaves. Women who were poor often worked with men on farms or in family businesses. Boys went to school. They studied math, reading, writing, and the arts. Some girls learned to read and write at home. They also learned to cook and sew.

> The Acropolis was a religious center in ancient Athens.

Ancient Rome

Long ago, Roman men worked outside the home while women took care of the home and children. Men who were wealthy worked in banking or in government. Women or servants taught girls at home. Boys usually went to a teacher's home to learn. Later in life, boys learned to do their fathers' jobs. Girls learned to care for the home and to make things that the family needed.

 **TextWork**

❸ What three subjects did boys in both ancient Athens and ancient Sumer study?

reading, writing, math

Rome

❹ Circle the name of the ancient community in which wealthy men worked in banking or in government.

> The Forum was a public square in ancient Rome. People met there to talk about government and business.

The United States in the 1800s

⑤ Circle two reasons many Americans moved west in the 1800s.

⑥ Underline the definition of *pioneers*.

⑦ List three things that made the journey west hard for pioneers.

_____

_____

_____

In the 1800s, many Americans moved west. Some wanted to find land for farming. Others wanted to find new jobs. **Pioneers**, or people who settle new lands, traveled in groups of covered wagons. The trip west was very hard. Pioneers faced problems such as sickness, accidents, and bad weather during the trip.

Once they found land to settle, pioneer men raised farm animals and planted crops. They also cut trees to get logs to build cabins. Women helped raise farm animals and took care of the home.

Children in History

Pioneer Children

Life on the trail was hard for young pioneers. Many children could not wear shoes because their feet were swollen from walking many miles each day. However, pioneer children found simple ways to have fun. They chased butterflies and grasshoppers. Games included I spy, hide-and-seek, leapfrog, and jump rope. Some pioneer children also read books at night by the light of a lantern.

Sweets were not very common. Eight-year-old Kate McDaniel wrote in her diary about cookies. "We would take a bite and nibble like mice. We would try to make them last as long as possible."

❯ Today, girls and boys in the United States go to school.

Boys and girls of some pioneer families went to school every day, except Sunday. During the summer, most children stayed home to help their families grow crops and raise farm animals. Boys would often grow up to continue their fathers' jobs. Girls would grow up to take care of their own homes and children.

The United States Today

The roles of men and women today are different from those in the past. Today, both men and women work outside the home. Both men and women take care of the home and children.

Most children today go to school. Also, it is no longer expected that boys will learn their fathers' jobs and that girls will work only inside the home.

 **TextWork**

❽ Look at Children in History on page 52. List one way pioneer children are the same as children today and one way they are different.

_____

_____

_____

❾ Underline examples of how people living in the United States today are different from people living in the United States in the past.

1. **SUMMARIZE** How have families changed over time?

_____

_____

_____

2. Why did **pioneers** want to move west?

_____

_____

_____

3. Why is it important to learn about people who lived long ago?

_____

_____

_____

4. How is your life different from the lives of boys and girls of ancient times?

_____

_____

_____

5. In what ways is your life like that of a pioneer child?

_____

_____

_____

_____

activity

Make a Poster Create a poster that shows the daily life of a child in another time and place.

Communities in Different Times and Places

Communities change over time. In the past, many communities were small. Some of them have remained small. However, other communities have grown as people and businesses have moved there from larger communities. **What do you think you will learn about communities in different times and places?**

_____

_____

Greensboro, North Carolina

**NORTH CAROLINA
STANDARD COURSE OF STUDY**

2.03 Describe similarities and differences among communities in different times and in different places.

TextWork

❶ Circle one reason that businesses long ago depended on railroads.

❷ What is an urban area?

_____

❸ What attracted thousands of people to Charlotte in the 1920s?

texiyel meyeis

▶ **Present-day Charlotte, North Carolina**

Urban Communities

In the early 1800s, railroads were built to connect growing communities. Businesses needed railroads to move goods to sell in other communities. As businesses grew, communities located along railroad tracks grew, too. These communities soon became urban areas. An **urban** area is a city. Many cities today have busy streets and tall buildings.

In the early 1900s, urban communities grew quickly. By 1920, more than 300 textile mills had been built in Charlotte, North Carolina. These mills attracted thousands of people looking for jobs. Today, Charlotte is North Carolina's largest city.

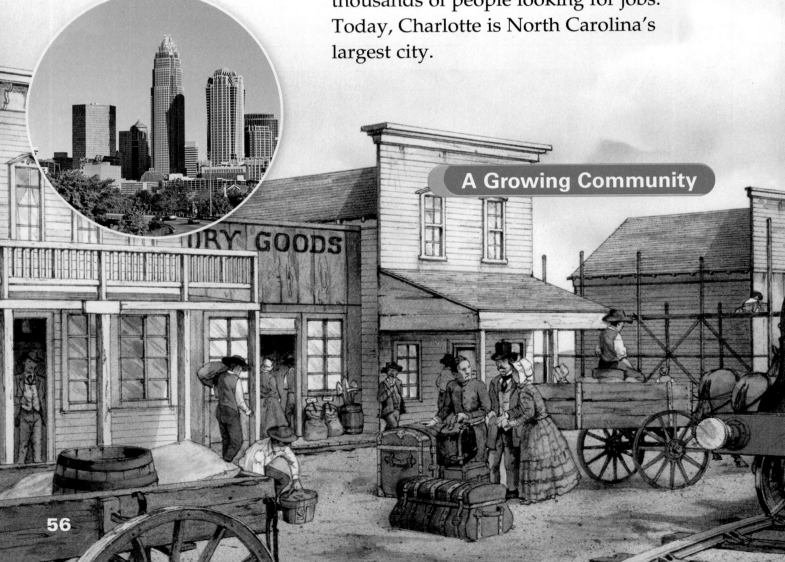

A Growing Community

Suburban Communities

In the 1950s, many people began moving from large cities to suburbs (SUH•berbz). A **suburb** is a smaller city or town near a large city. Today, many people live in the suburbs and work in urban areas. They may travel to work by train, by subway, or by car.

In the past, suburban areas often had few businesses. Today, many businesses are in the suburbs. These businesses are located closer to more people's homes.

Mint Hill is a suburb of Charlotte. Like Charlotte, Mint Hill has schools, stores, theaters, and doctors' offices. However, Charlotte offers people more choices.

TextWork

❹ Underline the definition of the word *suburb*.

❺ When did people begin moving to suburbs?

_1950's_

▶ A neighborhood in Mint Hill, North Carolina

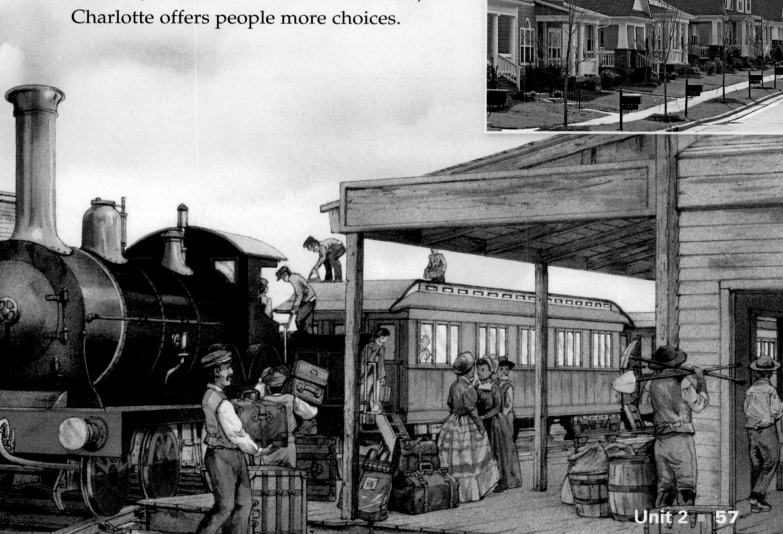

6 Write the definition of the word *rural*.

_____

_____

_____

7 Name one thing that people in rural areas did in the past that people continue to do there today.

_____

Rural Communities

Before railroads were built, most people lived in rural areas. **Rural** areas are in the countryside, away from cities and large towns. Small towns, farms, fields, and woods make up rural areas. In the past, people who lived in rural communities grew their own food and raised their own farm animals. Most children studied at home. Today, many rural areas are made up of farms that grow food for other communities.

Rockwell is a rural community outside of Charlotte. About 2,000 people live there. Some people who live in Rockwell work in Charlotte.

Communities in North Carolina

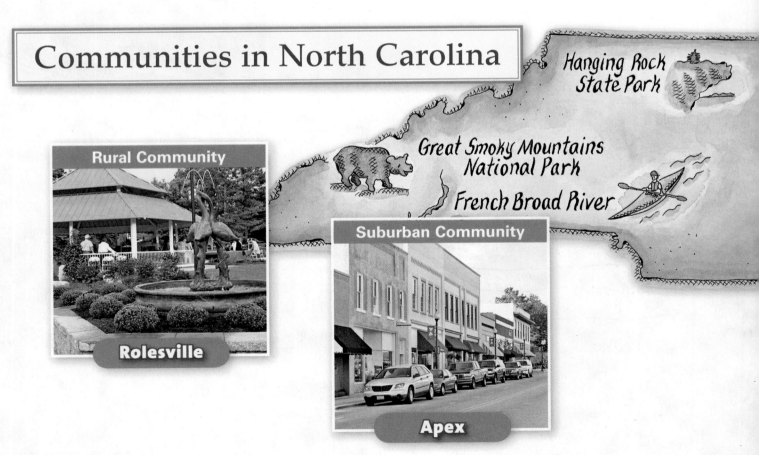

Hanging Rock State Park

Great Smoky Mountains National Park

French Broad River

Rural Community

Rolesville

Suburban Community

Apex

Community Links

Urban, suburban, and rural communities are important to one another. Rural areas produce food and other goods used in large cities. Suburbs provide quiet communities for people who want to work in cities but not live in them. Urban areas offer many choices for jobs, shopping, entertainment, education, and health care. Today, most people in the United States live in urban and suburban communities.

Raleigh is an urban community and the state capital. Apex is a suburb of Raleigh. Many people live in Apex but work in Raleigh. Rolesville is a rural community outside of Raleigh. People in Rolesville may drive to Raleigh to shop or to visit hospitals.

8 List two reasons people living in rural areas might need or want to visit urban areas.

_____

_____

9 Underline one urban area, one suburb, and one rural area of North Carolina.

10 Look at the photographs of the communities below. Circle the picture that is most like your community.

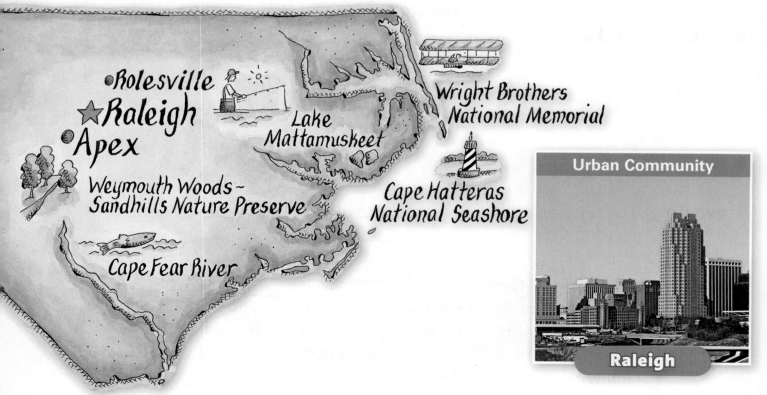

Urban Community

Raleigh

1. SUMMARIZE How have communities changed over time? How have they stayed the same?

_____

_____

_____

2. How is a **suburb** different from an **urban** area?

_____

_____

_____

3. Why do you think people live in suburbs today?

_____

_____

_____

4. Why do you think rural communities are important?

_____

_____

_____

MATCHING Draw a line to match the community on the left with its features on the right.

5. urban   a small community
                                      in the countryside

6. rural   a town near a large city

7. suburb   a city with tall buildings

writing

Write an Article Write an article about your community. Tell whether it is in an urban, suburban, or rural area. Describe your community and tell what it is like to live there.

Review and Test Prep

Unit 2

The Big Idea

People have different roles in families, at work, and in communities.

Summarize the Unit

 **Summarize** Complete the graphic organizer to show what you have learned about the roles people have in families, at work, and in communities.

Key Facts

Men, women, and children have had roles in families and communities throughout history.

The roles of men, women, and children have changed over time.

Summary

_____

_____

_____

_____

Use Vocabulary

Draw a line connecting each term with its definition.

1. community of people connected by similar ways of life

economy, p. 44

2. people who settle lands

society, p. 46

3. the ways people make and use goods and services

pioneers, p. 52

4. a smaller city or town near a large city

suburb, p. 57

Unit 2 ▪ 61

Think About It

5. What are the social roles of adults?

_____

_____

6. Why do you think towns grew after roads and railroads came to them?

_____

_____

7. How are rural, suburban, and urban communities connected?

_____

_____

Circle the letter of the correct answer.

8. Which is an economic role of American children today?

   A going to work

   B being a student

   C making origami

   D saving money

9. Which might you see in a rural community?

   A busy streets

   B farmlands

   C subway systems

   D tall buildings

Show What You Know

Writing Write a Paragraph
Explain the roles of family members in ancient times.

Activity Make a Mural
Make a mural to show roles that people have in families, at work, and in a community.

GO online To play a game that reviews the unit, join Eco in North Carolina Adventures online or on CD.

People and Communities Over Time

> Dr. Martin Luther King, Jr., at Lincoln Memorial, Washington, D.C.

Spotlight on Goals and Objectives

North Carolina Interactive Presentations

NORTH CAROLINA STANDARD COURSE OF STUDY

COMPETENCY GOAL 3 The learner will examine how individuals can initiate change in families, neighborhoods, and communities.

💡 The Big Idea

How can people change families, neighborhoods, and communities over time?

The actions of people affect the ways in which families, neighborhoods, and communities change over time. These changes can take place quickly or happen over several years. Families grow and change as people are born into them. They also change when people move far away. Neighborhoods and communities grow and change as people move to them. They change when people start new businesses and tear down old buildings. Events that happened long ago have changed families, neighborhoods, and communities. What happens today may affect the future, or the time still to come.

Think about what the word *change* means. Then describe how each event below would bring about change.

A family has a baby. _____

_____

_____

A new home is built in a neighborhood. _____

_____

_____

A new shopping mall is built in a community. _____

_____

_____

Reading Social Studies

 ## Sequence

❯ Learn

- **Sequence** is the order in which events happen.
- Words such as *first, next, then, last, after,* and *finally* are sequence clues.
- Sometimes events are not listed in the order in which they happened.

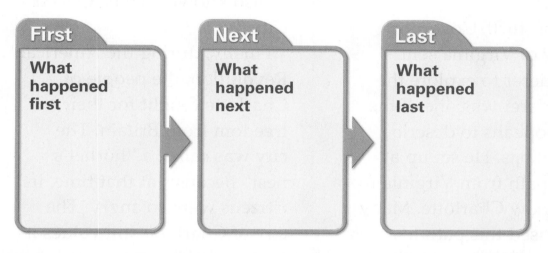

First	**Next**	**Last**
What happened first	What happened next	What happened last

❯ Practice

Circle four sequence clues in the paragraph below.

At first, people in North Carolina worked in gold mines during the 1800s. Next, people in North Carolina began growing cotton. Then, they built railroads near cities, such as Charlotte. The city of Charlotte became larger. Finally, Charlotte became a center for many banks and businesses. It is now the largest city in North Carolina.

Sequence

Read the following paragraphs.

Charlotte—The Queen City

What is now the city of Charlotte, North Carolina, has a long history. First, a group of American Indians, called the Catawba, lived in the area.

Next, in 1670, Governor Berkeley of Virginia sent John Lederer to explore the area. Lederer was one of the first Europeans to describe the Carolinas. He set up a trading path from Virginia to what is now Charlotte. Many settlers used this path to reach Charlotte.

Then, in 1755, settlers started building what would become downtown Charlotte. The city was named after Queen Charlotte of Britain. Charlotte is also known as the "Queen City."

Finally, during the American Revolution, the people of Charlotte fought for their freedom from Britain. The city was called a "hornet's nest" because, at that time, its citizens were so angry. The city of Charlotte still values its freedom today.

Add facts to show the sequence of events in Charlotte's history.

First	Next	Last
The Catawba lived in the area that is now the city of Charlotte.		

Families Over Time

1

Over time, some of the roles of family members have changed. In the past, men and women had certain roles. Today, men and women may have several roles in a family. **What might you learn about the roles of family members?**

_____

_____

▶ **Over time families have celebrated events together.**

NORTH CAROLINA STANDARD COURSE OF STUDY

3.03 Compare and contrast the family structure and the roles of its members over time.

TextWork

1 Look at the pictures on this page. List one thing that is different about the picture of the past and the picture of today.

_____

_____

2 Circle in the text ways in which family structures have changed over time.

❯ In the past, most women worked at home.

Family Structure

In the past, most families included a mother, a father, and their children. Today, some families have only one parent. In other families, children may have stepparents, stepbrothers, and stepsisters. In some families, several generations live in the same home. A **generation** is a group of people about the same age. The most important thing about any family is that its members take care of one another.

Roles of Adults

In the past, women mostly worked at home and raised their children. Few women went to college or had jobs. Men worked to earn money to support their families. Today, many women go to college and work at jobs. Many men help take care of their homes and children.

❯ Today, many women work in jobs outside of the home.

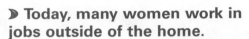

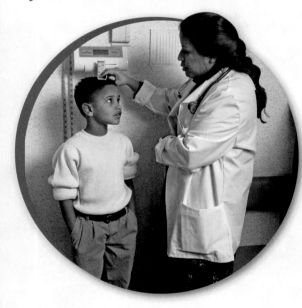

Roles of Children

In the past, many children worked with their parents. Girls helped their mothers with household chores and looked after younger children. Boys helped their fathers hunt, grow food, and raise animals. Children did not have as much time for school or play.

In the 1800s, many men and women began to work in mines and factories. Children often did, too, to help their families. They worked long hours for very little pay.

Today, most children go to school and do chores at home. As they get older, they may be given more responsibilities in the family. As they become young adults, they may begin working at part-time jobs.

TextWork

❸ Look at the pictures on this page. What do they show about how children in the past and children today are the same?

_____

_____

_____

❯ In the past, boys helped their fathers at work (left). Today, children help do chores at home (inset).

1. **SUMMARIZE** How have the roles of family members changed over time?

_____

_____

_____

_____

2. Write a sentence using the word **generation**.

_____

_____

_____

3. List two examples of how family structure today is different from family structure in the past.

_____

_____

_____

4. Why did children in the past not have as much free time as children do today?

_____

_____

_____

Circle the letter of the correct answer.

5. Which is a role of most children in families living in the United States today?

   A raising children

   B working in factories

   C going to school

   D working in mines

writing

✏ **Write a Narrative** Imagine that you are a child living in the past. Write a narrative about a day in your life.

Communities Over Time

2

Over time, communities have changed. Change can take place over a week, a month, a year, or several years. Communities continue to change today. They may grow in size as people and businesses move there. **What will you learn about ways communities change over time?**

_____

_____

▶ **Trade Street, Winston, North Carolina, in the early 1900s**

**NORTH CAROLINA
STANDARD COURSE OF STUDY**

3.01 Analyze changes which have occurred in communities past and present.

Winston-Salem

> ▶ An early nineteenth century painting of Main Street in Salem, North Carolina (above). Single Brothers' House (below)

The city of Winston-Salem began as two separate towns. They were known as Winston and Salem.

In 1766, a group of German-speaking immigrants called Moravians founded the settlement of Salem. A **settlement** is a new community. The Moravian Church owned all of the property that made up Salem.

At first, many families lived together in the same house. In time, people in Salem began building houses for each family. When boys and girls were 14 years old, they left their parents' houses. The girls lived in the Single Sisters' House. The boys lived in the Single Brothers' House. At first, only Moravians could live in Salem. After 1861, anyone could live there.

In 1849, the town of Winston was founded. In 1874, Joshua Reynolds started a tobacco company in Winston that created hundreds of jobs. Workers were also needed for furniture and fabric businesses. As people moved to Winston to find work, the town grew.

Because Salem and Winston were only one mile apart, community leaders wanted to join them. In 1889, the post offices for the two towns were combined. In 1913, the two towns were joined and renamed Winston-Salem. The new town became known as the Twin City.

Today, Winston-Salem is one of the largest cities in North Carolina. More than 185,000 people live there. Winston-Salem has become an important research center for technology and medicine. It also has several colleges, including Wake Forest University, Winston-Salem State University, and Salem College.

❯ Winston-Salem continues to grow and change as new people and businesses move there.

TextWork

❶ Underline the definition of *settlement*.

❷ Which town was founded first—Winston or Salem?

_____

❸ Underline the reason that leaders wanted to join the towns of Winston and Salem.

❹ Look at the pictures on pages 72–73. List two features of Winston-Salem that have changed over time.

_____

_____

▶ People traveled to Charlotte by covered wagons. Sometimes, children could not ride in the wagon because it was full of goods, such as butter churns (inset).

Charlotte

In the mid-1700s, Charlotte began as a settlement along the Great Wagon Road. Many settlers came to Charlotte on this road to trade goods. A **settler** is a person who comes to live in a new community.

Farming was an important business in Charlotte. Parents and children worked together on their farms. Over time, many people began growing enough crops that they had extra to sell. Some families hired workers to care for the crops. As a result, the children had more time for school.

In 1799, a farmer's son found a 17-pound piece of gold just east of Charlotte. Miners and other workers soon moved to the area in hopes of finding gold. People began to keep their money and gold safe in banks that opened in Charlotte.

TextWork

5 Write a sentence using the word *settler*.

_____

_____

_____

6 Underline in the text how the discovery of gold changed Charlotte.

During the mid-1850s, railroad companies built tracks through Charlotte. The railroads brought more growth and change. After 1870, factories called cotton mills were opened. The mills spun cotton into thread for making cloth. By the 1900s, Charlotte had many more new businesses, such as pipe and brick factories and department stores.

The banking business also grew and changed over time. Today, banking is the biggest business in Charlotte. In fact, the city is the second-largest center for banking in the United States. Many people in Charlotte work in banks. The city continues to change as more banks open and more people move to the city.

TextWork

7 Circle the event that happened first in Charlotte—the building of railroad tracks or the opening of cotton mills.

8 What is Charlotte's biggest business today? Underline the answer in the text.

9 Look at the pictures on pages 74–75. Circle things in the pictures that are different from people and communities today.

❯ Intersection of Trade Street and Tryon Street in Charlotte, North Carolina, in 1904

1. **SUMMARIZE** How do communities change and stay the same over time?

_____

_____

_____

2. Who founded the **settlement** of Salem?

_____

_____

3. Why do you think it is important to learn about how communities have changed over time?

_____

_____

_____

4. Why did people use the first banks in Charlotte?

_____

_____

_____

_____

Circle the letter of the correct answer.

5. What is true about Winston-Salem today?

   A People who live there own a lot of gold.

   B It is an important research center for technology and medicine.

   C It is known for its large banking businesses.

   D It is two separate cities.

activity

🖍 **Make a Travel Brochure** Make a travel brochure about one of the cities you learned about in this lesson. Illustrate ways the city has changed and stayed the same over time.

Review and Test Prep

The Big Idea

People in families, neighborhoods, and communities change over time.

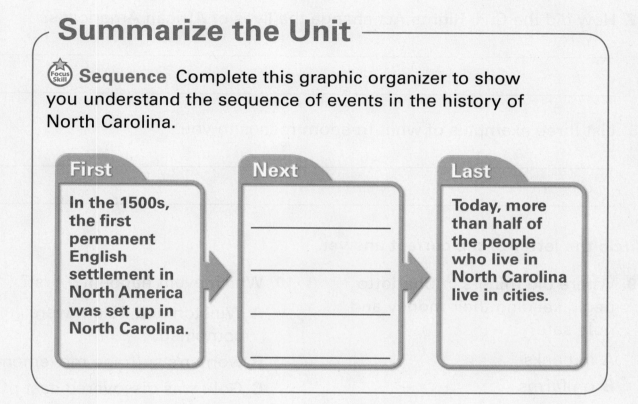

Summarize the Unit

Sequence Complete this graphic organizer to show you understand the sequence of events in the history of North Carolina.

First

In the 1500s, the first permanent English settlement in North America was set up in North Carolina.

Next

_____

_____

_____

_____

Last

Today, more than half of the people who live in North Carolina live in cities.

Use Vocabulary

Draw a line connecting each term with its definition.

1. a new community

   generation, p. 68

2. one of the first people to live in a new community

   settlement, p. 72

3. a person who comes to live in a country from somewhere else in the world

   settler, p. 74

4. a person who goes to find out about a place

   explorer, p. 78

5. a group of people of about the same age

   immigrant, p. 80

6. What did the Nineteenth Amendment do?

_____

_____

7. How did the Civil Rights Act change the lives of African Americans?

_____

_____

8. List three examples of what freedom means to you.

_____

_____

Circle the letter of the correct answer.

9. Where did miners in Charlotte begin keeping their money and gold safe?

   A in banks

   B on farms

   C in covered wagons

   D at colleges

10. Which event happened first?

   A Winston and Salem were combined.

   B woman's suffrage movement

   C Gold was discovered east of Charlotte.

   D American Revolution

Show What You Know

✏️ **Writing** **Write a Summary**
Describe some of the differences between families of long ago and families of today.

🖌️ **Activity** **Make a Time Line**
Make a time line of events in American history that have changed the ways in which people live. Illustrate each event.

GO online or on CD.

To play a game that reviews the unit, join Eco in North Carolina Adventures online

Our Geography

▷ A waterway in North Carolina

Spotlight on Goals and Objectives

North Carolina Interactive Presentations

 NORTH CAROLINA STANDARD COURSE OF STUDY

COMPETENCY GOAL 4 The learner will explain geographic concepts and the relationship between people and geography in real life situations.

💡 The Big Idea

How does geography affect the people living in an area?

The geography of every community is different. To describe a community's geography, a person would probably begin with its land and water. A community might be on flat land or near mountains. It might be near a river, a lake, or an ocean.

The types of land and water in an area affect the ways in which people get from place to place. They also affect the kinds of activities people do and the kinds of goods and services available.

In turn, people can affect an area. They may change the land and water of an area to meet their needs. They build roads, bridges, and tunnels. Every community is different, so the ways of life of the people living in it are different.

Think about the people and geography of your community. Then write a sentence to answer each question below.

What types of land and water are near your community? _____

_____

How do land and water affect people in

your community? _____

_____

How do people affect the land and water in

your community? _____

_____

Reading Social Studies

 ### Compare and Contrast

> ## Learn

- To **compare** and **contrast** people, ideas, and things is to tell how they are alike and different.
- Words and phrases such as *the same as, like, both,* and *similar* are clues that two things are being compared.
- Words and phrases such as *different from, unlike, however,* and *but* are clues that two things are being contrasted.

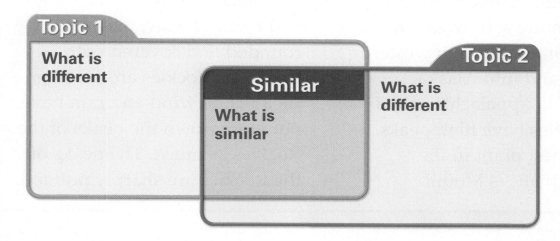

> ## Practice

Underline one sentence in the paragraph below that tells how the Appalachian Mountains and the Rocky Mountains are similar.

The Appalachian Mountains and the Rocky Mountains are the largest mountain ranges in the United States. The Appalachian Mountains are in the eastern United States. The Rocky Mountains are in the western United States.

Topic 1
Topic 2

Apply

Read the following paragraphs.

The Appalachians and the Rockies

The Appalachian Mountains and the Rocky Mountains both run through the United States and Canada. The Appalachian Mountains, or Appalachians, run from central Alabama into southeastern Canada. The Rocky Mountains, or Rockies, run from the southwestern United States through western Canada and into Alaska.

Both the Appalachians and the Rockies have high peaks. The highest point in the Appalachians is Mount Mitchell, at 6,684 feet. The highest point in the Rockies is Mount Elbert, at 14,433 feet.

Both mountain ranges are thousands of years old. Over time, wind and rain have changed their shapes. The Appalachians were once rough and rocky. Today, they are rounded and covered with trees. The Rockies are younger. As a result, wind and rain have not worn down the peaks of the Rockies as much. The peaks of the Rockies are sharply pointed.

What can you add to the chart below?

Appalachians

_____

_____

_____

_____

_____

Similar

They both run through the United States and Canada. Both are thousands of years old.

Rockies

_____

_____

_____

_____

_____

The Physical Environment

Every community has its own **physical environment**, or physical features. When people describe a community's physical environment, they talk about its land, water, plant life, and climate. **Climate** is the weather a place has over a long period of time. **What do you think you will learn about the physical environments of communities?**

_____

_____

❯ **The Appalachian Mountains, North Carolina**

NORTH CAROLINA STANDARD COURSE OF STUDY

4.03 Use geographic terminology to describe and explain variations in the physical environment of communities.

Landforms

❶ What is the difference between a valley and a plateau?

_____

_____

_____

❷ List the three regions of North Carolina.

_____

_____

_____

❸ **REGIONS** Circle the largest region of North Carolina on the map below.

One way to describe the physical environment is to talk about landforms. A **landform** is a kind of land, such as a plain or a mountain. A plain is flat land. A mountain range, or ridge, is a chain of mountains. Valleys and plateaus (pla•TOHZ) are also landforms. A valley is a low area of land between hills or mountains. A plateau has steep sides that rise to a flat top.

Landforms of North Carolina

North Carolina can be divided into three regions, based on the types of landforms in each one. A **region** is an area with at least one feature that makes it different from other areas. North Carolina's regions are the Mountain, the Piedmont, and the Coastal Plain.

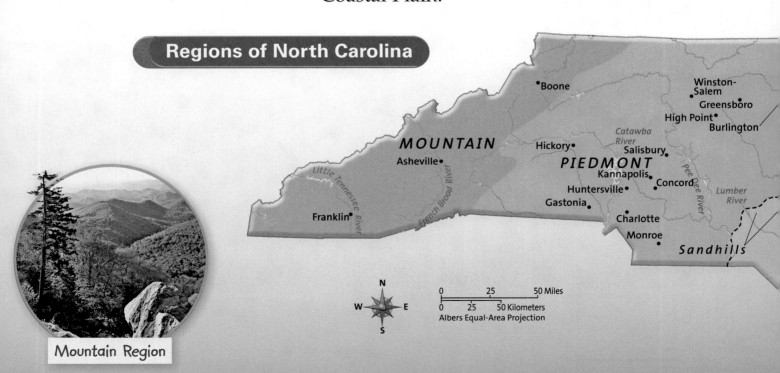

Mountain Region

The Mountain region has many forests and mountains. The Appalachian Mountains run through this region. The Appalachian Mountains are made up of many smaller mountain ranges. Both the Great Smoky Mountains and the Black Mountains are part of the Appalachian Mountains.

The Piedmont region is hilly. *Piedmont* means "at the foot of the mountain." The land is between 300 feet high in the eastern part of the region and 1,500 feet high in the western part. There are meadows and forests in this region.

The Coastal Plain is the largest land region. The land is flat with a few hills. The Coastal Plain also has swamps, wetlands, and forests.

❯ Dr. Elisha Mitchell measured the highest mountain east of the Mississippi River. This mountain, Mount Mitchell, is in North Carolina. It is 6,684 feet high.

Coastal Plain Region

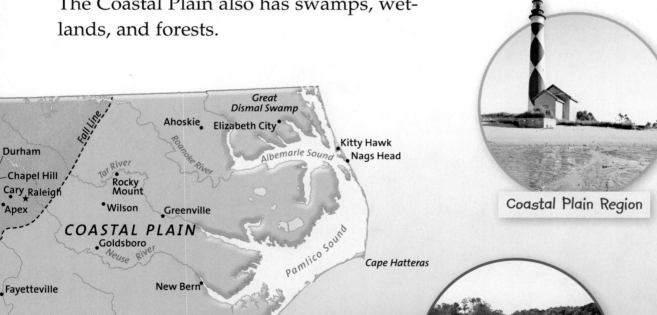

Piedmont Region

4 How are lakes, ponds, rivers, and streams alike?

_____

_____

5 Look at the illustration below. Circle the kinds of bodies of water that are near your community.

6 Underline the text that describes what a dam is. Circle an example of a dam in North Carolina.

Bodies of Water

Bodies of water also make up the physical environment of communities. Many communities are near bodies of water. Some communities may be near oceans. Oceans are the largest bodies of water and cover more than half of Earth. All ocean water is salty.

Lakes, ponds, rivers, and streams are all smaller bodies of water. You might describe a community as being near a lake or a river. Most of these bodies of water contain fresh water. Fresh water is water that is not salty. After it is treated, fresh water is the water we use in our homes and to drink.

Bodies of Water

Waterfall ——

—— River

Wetlands

Bodies of Water in North Carolina

Most rivers in North Carolina start in the Mountain or Piedmont region. From there, the rivers flow southeast and empty into the Atlantic Ocean.

A fall line forms the border between the Piedmont and the Coastal Plain. A **fall line** is where a river drops from higher to lower ground. Most rivers that cross a fall line have rapids or waterfalls.

North Carolina has natural and human-made lakes. Natural lakes are formed by nature. Human-made lakes are made by people. Dams form many human-made lakes. A **dam** is a structure built on a river to control the flow of water and to prevent floods. The Cowans Ford Dam formed Lake Norman in the Piedmont. Lake Norman is the largest human-made lake located entirely in North Carolina.

❯ Both Whitewater Falls (above) and the Cape Fear River (below) are in North Carolina.

— Stream

Lake —

▶ The Great Smoky Mountains (above) have a different climate from that of the Cape Hatteras National Seashore (inset).

Climate

Every community has a climate. The community's climate might be hot or cold. It might change from season to season. The community might be in a rainy place, or it might be very dry.

Earth and the Sun

A community's location on Earth affects its climate. Sunlight hits Earth at different angles in different places. Sunlight is most direct near the equator. Places closer to the equator are hotter and wetter than places farther away from it.

North Carolina's Climate

North Carolina is hot in the summer and cold in winter. It gets colder in the Mountain region than in the Piedmont and the Coastal Plain regions.

TextWork

7 How is the climate of places that are near the equator different from the climate of other places?

_____

_____

_____

8 Which region of North Carolina experiences the coldest weather?

_____

In August, the temperature in the Mountain region is about 65 degrees. In January, it is about 30 degrees. In the Coastal Plain the temperature can be more than 90 degrees in August and about 45 degrees in January.

North Carolina gets a lot of rain and snow. Sometimes, there are large storms called hurricanes. These storms form over the Atlantic Ocean. Hurricanes have heavy rains and strong winds. These storms can cause a lot of damage. Several strong hurricanes have hit the Coastal Plain of North Carolina.

 **TextWork**

9 Look at the bar graph below. What is the difference between the average precipitation in March and the average precipitation in November?

_____

10 Look at the bar graph below. In which month does Wilmington have the most precipitation?

_____

❯ A bar graph uses bars to show amounts. This bar graph compares the number of inches of precipitation in Wilmington during different months of the year.

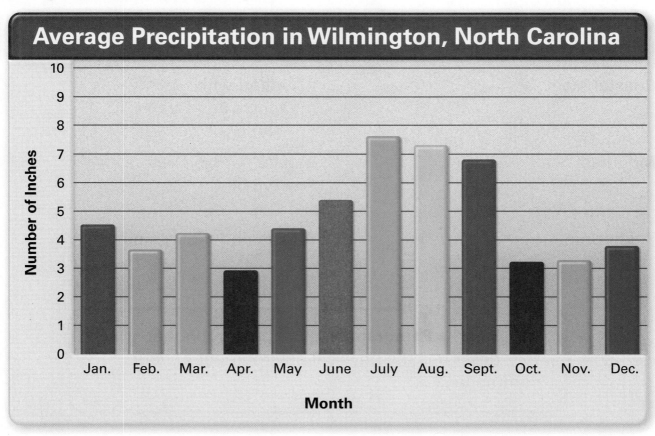

Average Precipitation in Wilmington, North Carolina

1. **SUMMARIZE** How do people describe physical environments?

_____

_____

2. Describe the Mountain **region** of North Carolina, using the word **landform**.

_____

_____

_____

3. What is the climate like in your community?

_____

_____

_____

4. How are the climates of the Coastal Plain region and the Piedmont region the same?

_____

_____

_____

MATCHING **Draw a line connecting each region of North Carolina on the left with the correct description on the right.**

5. Coastal Plain

hilly land with meadows and forests

6. Mountain

mostly flat land with a few hills

7. Piedmont

forests and mountains

writing

✎ **Write a Paragraph** Write a paragraph that describes the physical environment of your community.

People and the Environment

Every environment affects how people live. People **adapt**, or change, their ways of life to fit the environment. People also affect the environment. Sometimes, people **modify**, or change, the environment to meet their needs. **What do you think you will learn about how people adapt to and modify the environment?**

_____

_____

The Blue Ridge Parkway near Linville, North Carolina

NORTH CAROLINA STANDARD COURSE OF STUDY

4.04 Compare how people in different communities adapt to or modify the physical environment to meet their needs.

TextWork

❶ How are drivers affected by mountainous areas?

_____

_____

_____

❷ Underline seven examples of things people can do for fun in North Carolina, based on their community's environment.

▶ **People in North Carolina enjoy outdoor activities such as white-water rafting (inset) and hiking.**

People in the Environment

Today, people live in many types of environments. The physical environment often affects where people choose to live. The environment can also affect how they live. In mountainous areas, drivers have to travel slowly on steep and curving roads. In cold climates, they need engine heaters to start their cars.

What people do for fun can depend on their community's environment. In North Carolina, people who live in the Coastal Plain region may go to the beach. People in the Piedmont region may go boating, fishing, or horseback riding. People who live in the Mountain region may hike, ski, or snowboard.

Adapting to the Environment

People adapt their ways of life to fit their environments. Homes all over the world are built for the environment in which they are located. In desert communities, rocks and sand make up the yards. In communities along waterways, some people live on boats.

In the Mountain region of North Carolina, winters can be cold. People who live there wear warm clothing and burn fuels, such as oil and coal, to heat their homes in the winter months. In the summer, temperatures in the Coastal Plain and the Piedmont regions are warm. People wear lightweight clothing and sometimes use air-conditioning to keep cool.

❸ Underline two examples of how people adapt to the environment of the Mountain region.

❹ Circle an example of how people adapt to the environment of the Coastal Plain and Piedmont regions.

▶ The Mountain region is home to many ski resorts, such as Sugar Mountain (inset).

5 Why do people use irrigation?

_____

_____

6 Where does most farming in North Carolina take place?

_____

_____

_____

Modifying the Environment

People modify the environment to meet their needs or to do their jobs. Farmers and mining businesses modify the land to use natural resources. A **natural resource** is something from nature that people can use, such as water, soil, and trees.

Farming

To grow crops, people may need to clear land. Then they plow, or turn over the soil, to plant seeds. People have found ways to farm dry land and to water their crops during dry weather. They use irrigation to water their crops. **Irrigation** is the moving of water to dry areas.

Most farming in North Carolina is in the Coastal Plain and Piedmont regions. Some of the state's crops are cotton, soybeans, peaches, apples, and sweet potatoes.

➤ **Farmers in Rowan County, North Carolina, use irrigation to water tomato plants.**

▶ Mount Airy, North Carolina, has one of the largest open-pit granite quarries in the United States (above). Some miners work underground (inset).

Mining

People build mines to get minerals from beneath Earth's surface. People in North Carolina's Mountain region mine stone and gravel. People in North Carolina also mine emeralds, a valuable gemstone.

Some mines are dug deep into the ground. Others, called open-pit mines, are dug into the surface by machines. Open-pit mines are used to get stone from the land. Stone is used for making buildings and roads. Gravel is spread over roads before they are paved.

 TextWork

❼ Circle three examples of minerals that are mined in North Carolina.

❽ Underline the text that explains how stone is used.

9 Circle the word *reservoir,* and underline its definition.

10 Name one dam located in North Carolina.

_____

Human Features

People modify the land by adding **human features**, such as homes, dams, bridges, tunnels, canals, and roads.

Water and Electricity

Communities modify the land to control the flow of water. In some areas, people build dams across rivers.

In 1944, work began on Fontana Dam, in western North Carolina. This dam made Fontana Lake, which is a large reservoir (REH•zuh•vwar). A **reservoir** is a human-made lake that collects and stores water.

People also build dams to make power. Water falling through a dam turns machines to make electricity called hydroelectric power. *Hydro* means "water." Fontana Dam makes hydroelectric power for people living in North Carolina.

Transportation

Today, people have added roads, bridges, and railroads to the environment to improve transportation. **Transportation** is the moving of people or things from one place to another. Many people in North Carolina helped build the Blue Ridge Parkway. It lets people drive through the mountains of North Carolina and Virginia.

Tunnels are another way to improve transportation. A **tunnel** is a path that runs under or through the land. To complete the Blue Ridge Parkway, people built tunnels through the mountains.

Like tunnels, canals make travel distances shorter. A **canal** is a waterway dug across land. In North Carolina, canals near the Atlantic Ocean form part of the Atlantic Intracoastal Waterway. This waterway lets people ship goods to places that they might not be able to reach by land.

TextWork

11 Circle the name of the road that people use to travel through the mountains of North Carolina and Virginia.

12 Where are canals located in North Carolina?

_____

_____

❯ The Atlantic Intracoastal Waterway runs from Massachusetts to Florida.

1. **SUMMARIZE** In what ways do people adapt to and modify the physical environment?

_____

_____

_____

_____

_____

_____

2. Use the words **tunnel** and **canal** in a sentence about **transportation**.

_____

_____

_____

_____

3. How do farmers modify the land?

_____

_____

_____

4. How does a dam help create power?

_____

_____

_____

Circle the letter of the correct answer.

5. What is a reservoir?

   A the moving of water to dry land

   B a waterway dug across land

   C a human-made lake

   D a term that means "water"

activity

🖍 **Draw a Picture** With your classmates, list ways in which people have changed the environment where you live. Then make a picture of one of those changes. Write a caption for your picture.

Review and Test Prep

 ## The Big Idea

Geography affects the people who live in an area.

Summarize the Unit

Compare and Contrast Complete the graphic organizer to compare and contrast the ways people in North Carolina adapt to the different regions.

Piedmont region

_____

_____

_____

_____

Similar

Both regions are located in North Carolina. They both have warmer climates than the mountain region.

Coastal Plain region

_____

_____

_____

_____

Use Vocabulary

Draw a line connecting each term with its definition.

1. a place's land, water, or plant life   **physical feature,** p. 94

2. buildings, roads, bridges, or canals   **latitude,** p. 103

3. the weather that a place has over a long time   **climate,** p. 105

4. imaginary lines on a map that run east and west   **human feature,** p. 118

Think About It

5. How would you describe your community's geography?

_____

_____

6. What geographic tools could you use to show someone the location of your community?

_____

_____

7. Describe the relative location of North Carolina.

_____

_____

Circle the letter of the correct answer.

8. Which of the following is a landform?

   A river

   B reservoir

   C mountain

   D canal

9. Which is a way that people modify the environment?

   A irrigation

   B fall lines

   C borders

   D rivers

Show What You Know

Writing Write a Poem
Describe your community's location. Give your poem a title, and make it at least four lines long.

Activity Make a Collage
Divide a sheet of paper into three sections, and label them *Coastal Plain*, *Mountain*, and *Piedmont*. Then cut and paste pictures that show physical features and human features of each region.

GO online or on CD.

To play a game that reviews the unit, join Eco in North Carolina Adventures online

People and Economics

Spotlight on Goals and Objectives

North Carolina Interactive Presentations

NORTH CAROLINA STANDARD COURSE OF STUDY

COMPETENCY GOAL 5 The learner will apply basic economic principles to the study of communities.

Charlotte, North Carolina, skyline

☀ The Big Idea

How do people in a community depend on one another to make, buy, and sell goods and services?

Think about how busy you would be if you had to make all the things you use. If you wanted to eat, you would have to grow your own vegetables or hunt and raise animals. If you wanted water, you would have to dig a well or carry water from a river or a lake. If you wanted to have a home, you would have to build it.

Early people had to make everything they used. As communities have grown over time, people have come to be able to share work with others. Today, members of communities depend on one another to work together to meet their needs. People count on farmers to grow food for them to eat or sell. They count on stores to sell clothes and other goods. They count on doctors and nurses to provide services that help them stay well. Workers in the community count on people to buy the goods and services they sell. Every member of each community is responsible for helping others meet their needs.

Write a description of a person who works in your community. Explain how people in your community depend on this person.

_____

_____

_____

Reading Social Studies

 Generalize

▶ Learn

- To generalize is to make a general statement based on what you know about a group of ideas.
- A generalization should be based on facts.
- To generalize, decide what the facts have in common.

Facts

Information given	Information given	Information given

Generalization

General statement about the information given

▶ Practice

Write a sentence that makes a generalization about the paragraph below.

In 1961, the Atlantic Coast Line Railroad moved its head- **Fact** quarters away from Wilmington, North Carolina. As a result, the city lost jobs and money. Community members were worried about the city's economy. They started businesses that would deliver goods and services to visitors.

_____

_____

Read the following paragraphs.

Tourism in Wilmington, North Carolina

Many people visit Wilmington, North Carolina. Visitors come to see the city's historic sites and museums. They enjoy the city's many beaches and gardens. They can also explore the battleship USS *North Carolina*.

Visitors can see the film and television studios of EUE Screen Gems Studios, too. More than 300 films, television shows, and commercials have been made there.

Visitors to Wilmington bring money into the city. They pay to stay in hotels. They buy meals at restaurants and goods in the city's stores. Visitors need services, too. These services create jobs in Wilmington. Some people work in hotels and restaurants. Others keep the visitor sites clean and safe.

Use the facts below to make a generalization.

Facts

Visitors come to see the historic sites and museums of Wilmington.	Visitors can see the film and television studios of EUE Screen Gems Studios.	Visitors who come to explore Wilmington bring money into the city.

Generalization

_____

_____

_____

Economic Resources

Businesses and factories use different economic resources to make and sell goods. An **economic resource** is something, such as a good or a service, that helps people meet their needs. Natural, human, and capital resources are all types of economic resources. **What will you learn about economic resources?**

_____

_____

▶ A market in New York City, New York

NORTH CAROLINA STANDARD COURSE OF STUDY

5.05 Distinguish and analyze the economic resources within communities.

▶ **Longleaf pines are an important economic resource.**

TextWork

❶ Circle five examples of natural resources in the text.

❷ Which raw material do businesses in Caldwell County, North Carolina, use to make products?

_____

❸ List four examples of nonliving resources.

_____

_____

_____

_____

Natural Resources

Natural resources are an important economic resource. Natural resources include water, soil, trees, farmland, and minerals.

Businesses use different natural resources to make goods and provide services. Some businesses begin with a raw material. A **raw material** is a natural resource that people can use to make a good. Some raw materials that businesses use are metal, rock, wood, and water.

In Caldwell County, North Carolina, many businesses use trees that grow in the western part of the state. After these trees are cut down, businesses use the wood to make furniture. Then they sell the furniture to the public.

Renewable and Nonrenewable Resources

There are different types of natural resources. Natural resources can be living or nonliving. Plants, trees, and wild animals are examples of living resources. Nonliving resources include water, metal, soil, and minerals.

A **renewable** resource can be made again by nature or people. Trees are renewable resources. After trees are cut down, new trees can be planted.

A **nonrenewable** resource cannot be made again quickly by nature or people. Minerals, such as emeralds found in North Carolina, are nonrenewable. It might take thousands of years for Earth to replace a mineral that has been used. Fuels, such as coal and oil are also nonrenewable. People burn fuels to make heat or energy.

❱ Oil is a nonrenewable resource found deep underground.

❹ How do businesses depend on human resources?

_____

_____

_____

❺ Underline four examples of ways that furniture businesses use human resources.

Human Resources

In addition to natural resources, businesses depend on human resources. **Human resources** are the workers who produce goods and services. Without human resources, natural resources could not be made into goods.

Furniture businesses need many human resources. In 2005, more than 58,000 people in North Carolina worked for businesses that made furniture. Some workers raise and cut down trees. Others use the wood to make furniture. Another group of workers sells the furniture in stores. Other workers deliver the furniture to customers.

A Furniture Factory

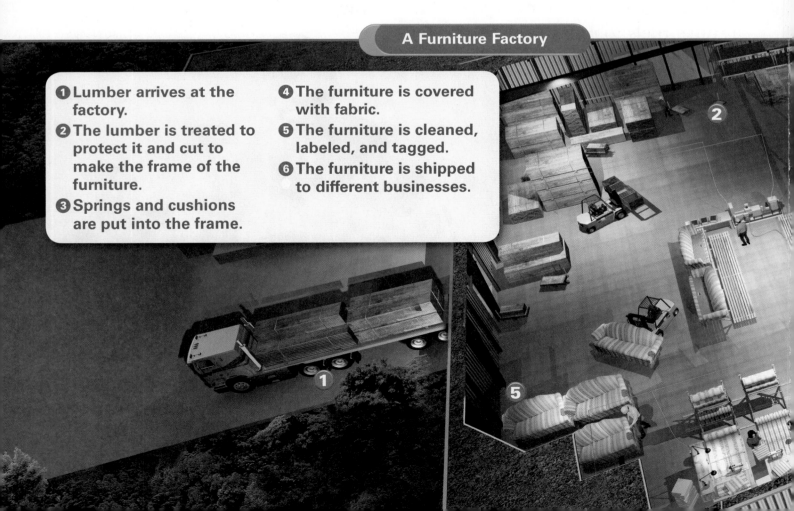

❶ Lumber arrives at the factory.

❷ The lumber is treated to protect it and cut to make the frame of the furniture.

❸ Springs and cushions are put into the frame.

❹ The furniture is covered with fabric.

❺ The furniture is cleaned, labeled, and tagged.

❻ The furniture is shipped to different businesses.

Capital Resources

Businesses also use **capital resources**, or tools and buildings. The factories where businesses make goods are capital resources. The machines used to make and deliver goods are also capital resources. Without these capital resources, furniture workers could not make furniture.

Money is a capital resource. People who want to open a business need money to start the business. In North Carolina, business leaders, such as William Henry Snow, used their own money to help the furniture business grow. With money, these business leaders could start companies, buy machines and buildings, and hire workers.

TextWork

6 Underline five examples of capital resources.

7 Why is money an important capital resource?

_____

_____

_____

➤ **William Henry Snow**

1. **SUMMARIZE** How do economic resources help people meet their needs?

_____

_____

_____

2. List three **economic resources** that businesses use.

_____

_____

_____

_____

3. How do furniture businesses use human resources?

_____

_____

_____

4. Why might a natural resource that is nonrenewable, such as emeralds in North Carolina, cost a lot of money?

_____

_____

_____

Circle the letter of the correct answer.

5. Which is an example of a renewable resource?

    A coal

    B oil

    C emerald

    D trees

activity

Make a Chart Choose a business in your community. Make a chart to show how it uses the three types of economic resources.

Economic Interdependence

Many goods you buy come from other communities. The way in which people depend on one another for goods and resources is called economic **interdependence**. Most communities show economic interdependence through trade. **Trade** is the exchange of one good or service for another. Trade lets people buy things that their own communities do not grow or make. **What will you learn about economic interdependence?**

_____

_____

An aerial view of the Port of Wilmington, North Carolina

**NORTH CAROLINA
STANDARD COURSE OF STUDY**

5.06 Recognize and explain reasons for economic interdependence of communities.

1 Circle the term *interstate trade*. Then underline an example of it in the text.

2 Name one example of how businesses in Kansas might use interstate trade.

_____

_____

_____

3 REGIONS Look at the map on page 135. Circle three goods made or grown near your community.

One Nation, Many Goods

North Carolina has many climates and natural resources. If you live in the Coastal Plain, your grocery store might sell fish caught off the coast of the Atlantic Ocean. But not all resources can be found in the Coastal Plain. Stores near the Coastal Plain may sell dairy products from the Piedmont region.

The entire United States has different climates and natural resources. People in each state use goods made or grown in other states. For example, North Carolinians might buy lobsters caught off the coast of Maine. People in Maine might buy cotton, sweet potatoes, or soybeans grown in North Carolina. Buying and selling between states is **interstate trade**.

▶ A farmers' market in Charlotte, North Carolina

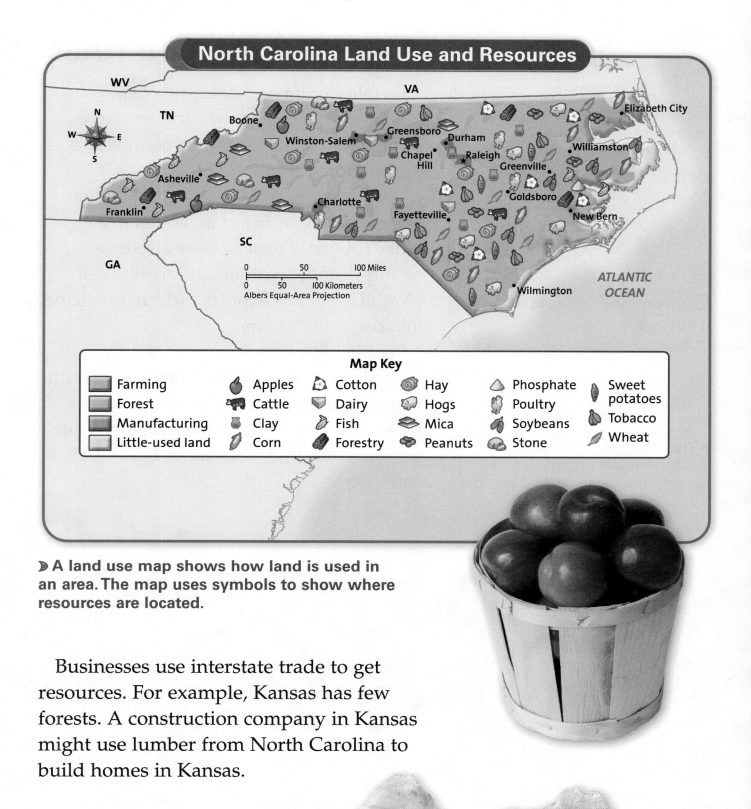

North Carolina Land Use and Resources

WV

VA

TN

Boone

Greensboro

Durham

Elizabeth City

Winston-Salem

Chapel Hill

Raleigh

Williamston

Asheville

Greenville

Franklin

Charlotte

Goldsboro

Fayetteville

New Bern

SC

GA

0   50   100 Miles

0   50   100 Kilometers
Albers Equal-Area Projection

Wilmington

ATLANTIC OCEAN

N E W S

Map Key

Farming	Apples	Cotton	Hay
Forest	Cattle	Dairy	Hogs
Manufacturing	Clay	Fish	Mica
Little-used land	Corn	Forestry	Peanuts

Phosphate	Sweet potatoes	
Poultry	Tobacco	
Soybeans	Wheat	
Stone		

▶ A land use map shows how land is used in an area. The map uses symbols to show where resources are located.

Businesses use interstate trade to get resources. For example, Kansas has few forests. A construction company in Kansas might use lumber from North Carolina to build homes in Kansas.

Trade Among Countries

People in different countries depend on one another for goods and resources. Buying and selling between countries is **international trade**.

People in countries such as the United States **import**, or bring in, goods from other countries to sell. They also **export**, or ship, goods to other countries to sell. North Carolina's exports include medicine, tobacco, and clothing.

People in Germany, Japan, and the United States export automobiles to South America and Africa. People in Germany, Japan, and the United States import fruit grown in South American and African countries.

❯ **This illustration shows some goods that are imported and exported throughout the world.**

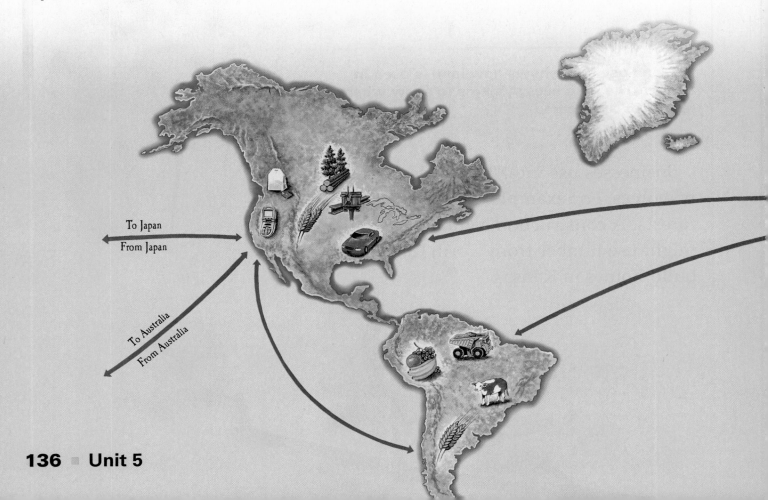

To Japan
From Japan

To Australia
From Australia

Countries also import and export resources that are used to make goods. For example, Canada exports wood that people use in many businesses across the United States.

People Are Interdependent

Supply and demand help make people interdependent. The products and services that businesses provide are the **supply**. People create the **demand**, or the willingness to buy goods and services.

People depend on one another to create a demand for goods and services. A company cannot stay in business if customers do not want what it sells. For example, in a town where there are few small children, a babysitting service will not have much success.

TextWork

❻ Underline three examples of countries that export automobiles.

❼ What is the difference between *supply* and *demand*?

_____

_____

_____

_____

_____

_____

_____

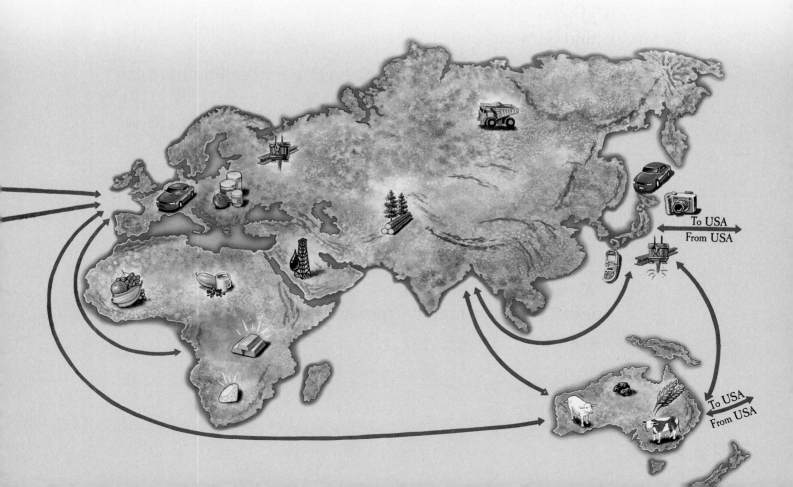

To USA
From USA

To USA
From USA

1. **SUMMARIZE** How do communities have economic interdependence?

_____

_____

_____

2. What is the difference between an **import** and an **export**?

_____

_____

_____

3. How do supply and demand make people interdependent?

_____

_____

_____

4. How does trade help people meet their needs?

_____

_____

_____

_____

Circle the letter of the correct answer.

5. Which best describes international trade?

   A buying and selling between states

   B buying and selling between countries

   C buying and selling between cities

   D buying and selling between families

activity

Make a Map Make a map to show how goods get to your community from around the world.

Specialization and Division of Labor

Today, specialization lets people buy many different kinds of goods and services. **Specialization** is doing one kind of work or selling one kind of good. The process of making goods and providing services is divided among workers. Dividing work so that each worker does part of a larger job is called **division of labor**. What will you learn about specialization and division of labor?

_____

_____

⟩ A factory worker in North Carolina

NORTH CAROLINA STANDARD COURSE OF STUDY

5.03 Apply concepts of specialization and division of labor to the local community.

5.04 Compare and contrast the division of labor in local and global communities.

Specialization

Colleges and other schools help prepare people for specialized jobs. For example, your teacher had to go to college to learn how to teach in a school. Others become experts at doing specialized work by doing the same job for a long time. Specialization lets businesses do only one type of thing, so they are able to do it well.

Many doctors **specialize**, or do all their work in one area of medicine. For example, some doctors specialize in caring for children. Other doctors specialize in caring for adults. Doctors who specialize in working with animals are called veterinarians.

▶ Teachers and veterinarians go to college to prepare for their specialized jobs.

Sometimes, workers and businesses have to change their specialization. In North Carolina, growing tobacco does not earn as much money as it once did. Some tobacco farmers have learned how to specialize in growing other kinds of crops. Some now raise organic, or naturally grown, fruits and vegetables. Sweet potatoes, soybeans, strawberries, and corn are some of the crops grown in North Carolina today.

TextWork

❶ Circle three examples of ways that people can prepare for specialized jobs.

❷ Look at the pictures on page 140. Circle two specialized jobs pictured.

❸ Underline four kinds of crops grown in North Carolina today.

▶ A garlic crop at an organic farm in North Carolina

4 Circle two ways that division of labor helps businesses.

5 How do farmers use division of labor?

_____

_____

_____

_____

Division of Labor in North Carolina

Without specialization, most division of labor would not be possible. Businesses get more work done more quickly by dividing work among workers. Because things can be done more quickly and easily, division of labor helps lower the price of goods and services.

Farming in North Carolina

Farming is one of the main businesses in North Carolina. Most farmers grow crops to sell to other communities. They use division of labor to get food from their farms to grocery stores and markets.

To begin, farmers use machines to plow the land and to help plant crops. On some farms, workers treat crops to keep insects and diseases from destroying them. Farmers then use machines to harvest crops that are ready to be picked.

▶ A worker picks the fruits from tomato plants (inset). Just picked tomatoes are sent by truck to be washed and cleaned (right).

After crops are picked, trucks take the food to factories. At the factories, workers wash and treat the food to preserve it. Preserving food keeps it from spoiling before it reaches grocery stores. Other workers sort and package the food. Drivers deliver the food to grocery stores and markets. Grocery and market workers then put it on shelves for people to buy.

Division of labor lets farmers grow large amounts of food quickly. Without it, communities might not have enough food to buy at grocery stores or markets.

Construction in North Carolina

Division of labor also is a part of construction work in North Carolina. Some workers pour the concrete that forms the floor of a building. Other workers build the walls and roofs.

After a building is completed, workers paint the walls. Others put in flooring. Construction workers divide these jobs so that they can build more quickly.

▶ Farm workers pick through tomatoes (top left). A grocery store worker puts out fresh tomatoes (above).

 TextWork

❻ Why is it better for the farming industry to use division of labor?

_____

_____

_____

❼ Circle four ways that construction workers use division of labor.

8 List two communities in different parts of the world that use division of labor.

_____

_____

9 **LOCATION** Look at the map below. Circle the countries that border Mozambique.

Division of Labor in Global Communities

Many communities use division of labor within their community. Other communities divide labor among workers across the world.

Farming in Manica

Manica (mah•NEE•kah) is a rural region in eastern Mozambique (moh•zahm•BEEK), a country in Africa. Some families in Manica are part of a farming cooperative. A **cooperative** is a group of workers who own a business together. Each worker in the group votes to help make decisions about the business.

Manica, Mozambique

DEM. REP. CONGO
TANZANIA
MALAWI
ANGOLA
ZAMBIA
MOZAMBIQUE
NAMIBIA
ZIMBABWE • Manica
BOTSWANA
MADAGASCAR
ATLANTIC OCEAN
SWAZILAND
SOUTH AFRICA
LESOTHO
INDIAN OCEAN

❯ A farmer raises chickens in Manica.

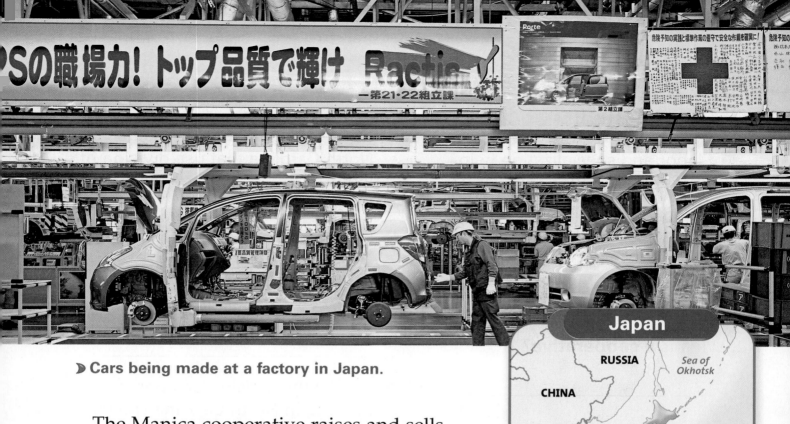

▶ **Cars being made at a factory in Japan.**

The Manica cooperative raises and sells chickens. The community divides the labor among families in the cooperative. Some families grow sunflowers, which are made into chicken feed. Others raise the chickens. Other families sell the chickens.

Japanese Automobile Manufacturing

Today, many automobiles are manufactured in Japan. To **manufacture** is to make goods by hand or by machine. Workers divide labor to manufacture automobiles. For example, some make engine parts. Others build engines. In the end, they put all of the pieces together to make automobiles. Many Japanese automobile makers are using division of labor on a global level. They are building and using factories in other countries, such as the United States. As a result, Japan can sell more automobiles in different parts of the world faster.

Japan

RUSSIA

Sea of Okhotsk

CHINA

NORTH KOREA

Sea of Japan (East Sea)

JAPAN

SOUTH KOREA

•Tokyo

PACIFIC OCEAN

East China Sea *Philippine Sea*

 TextWork

⑩ LOCATION Look at the map above. Circle the bodies of water near Japan.

⑪ Underline one way that Japan uses division of labor on a global level.

1. **SUMMARIZE** How do division of labor and specialization help communities around the world?

_____

_____

_____

2. What is a **cooperative**?

_____

_____

_____

3. How has specialization helped businesses?

_____

_____

_____

4. List two examples of industries in North Carolina that use division of labor.

_____

_____

_____

_____

5. How is the division of labor in farming in North Carolina similar to and different from the division of labor in farming in Manica?

_____

_____

_____

_____

_____

_____

writing

Write a Paragraph Write a paragraph about how businesses use specialization and division of labor in your community.

Scarcity and the Economy

The United States has a free enterprise economy. In a **free enterprise** economy, people can make or sell any good or service allowed by law. In order to earn money, businesses offer goods and services that meet people's demands. Sometimes there is plenty of a good or service. Other times there is scarcity. **Scarcity** means that the supply of a good or service is not enough to meet the demand for it. **What do you think you will learn about scarcity?**

_____

_____

▶ Crabtree Valley Mall, Raleigh, North Carolina

NORTH CAROLINA STANDARD COURSE OF STUDY

5.01 Define and identify examples of scarcity.

5.02 Explain the impact of scarcity on the production, distribution, and consumption of goods and services.

Scarcity

What consumers want helps businesses decide what to sell. Sometimes there is a high demand for a good or a service. For example, in a community with many pets, there may be a demand for pet-care goods and services. As a result, businesses may offer more of these goods and services. The demand for these goods and services may also affect their price.

Prices are also affected by the scarcity of a good or service. If there are not many people available to do a service, such as walking dogs, the price to get a dog walker may go up.

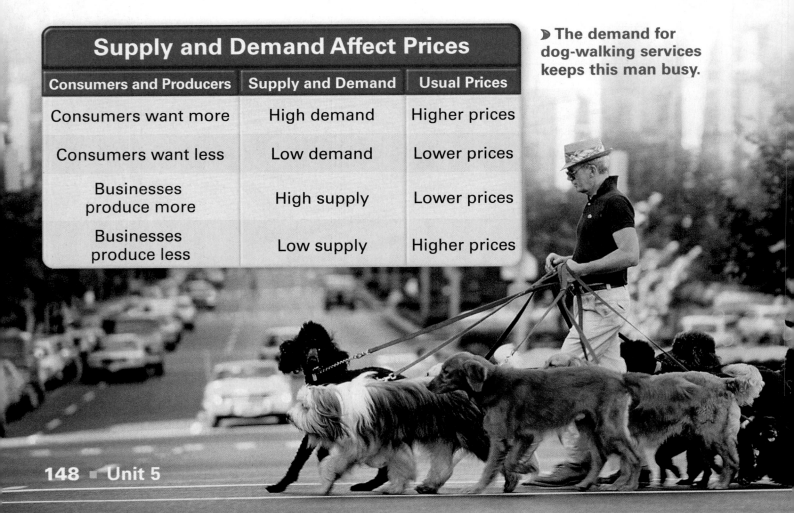

❯ The demand for dog-walking services keeps this man busy.

Supply and Demand Affect Prices		
Consumers and Producers	Supply and Demand	Usual Prices
Consumers want more	High demand	Higher prices
Consumers want less	Low demand	Lower prices
Businesses produce more	High supply	Lower prices
Businesses produce less	Low supply	Higher prices

> Today, four out of every ten sweet potatoes sold in the United States are grown in North Carolina.

Production

Businesses depend on producers to make goods and services. **Production** is the process of making goods and services.

Farmers in North Carolina produce more sweet potatoes than farmers in any other state in the United States. Almost half of the sweet potatoes in the United States come from North Carolina.

Suppose that dry weather destroys many of North Carolina's sweet potato crops. As a result, the production of sweet potatoes goes down. This decrease in production causes sweet potatoes to become scarce. When sweet potatoes become scarce, their price goes up.

 TextWork

❹ Circle the word *production*. Then underline its definition.

❺ How does scarcity affect price?

_____

_____

_____

_____

_____

TextWork

6 What happens to the distribution of a good if the production of the good increases?

_____

_____

_____

7 Circle one example of how scarcity affects distribution.

8 List one way that scarcity affects the consumption of a good.

_____

_____

_____

Distribution

Businesses depend on the distribution of goods. **Distribution** is the sending of goods to stores to be sold to consumers. If production of a good goes up, distribution of that good may also go up. If production of a good goes down, distribution of that good may also go down.

If sweet potatoes became scarce, their distribution might go down. As a result, there might not be enough sweet potatoes to send to stores. Certain grocery stores and markets might have only small amounts of sweet potatoes. Other grocery stores and markets might not have any sweet potatoes at all to sell.

▶ **A farmers' market in Raleigh, North Carolina**

Consumption

Scarcity sometimes affects **consumption**, or the use of goods and services. When a good or service is scarce, there is often not enough of the good or service available for people to buy. Scarcity can affect consumption if people choose not to buy scarce goods because the prices are too high.

If sweet potatoes are scarce, people might not be able to buy as many as they want. As a result, the consumption of sweet potatoes might go down. Some people might buy other foods, such as carrots or peas, instead of sweet potatoes. When people buy other foods, the consumption of those foods goes up.

▶ Scarcity of one food can cause the consumption of other foods to go up.

1. **SUMMARIZE** How does scarcity affect the production, distribution, and consumption of goods and services?

_____

_____

_____

_____

_____

2. What is the difference between **production** and **distribution**?

_____

_____

_____

_____

3. How does scarcity affect the price of a good or a service?

_____

_____

4. Why is it hard for people to buy scarce products?

_____

_____

_____

_____

Circle the letter of the correct answer.

5. Which of the following best describes the work of a farmer?

   A consumption

   B production

   C distribution

   D scarcity

writing

Write a Summary Describe how scarcity would affect the production, distribution, and consumption of sweet potatoes in North Carolina.

People and the Economy

Lesson 5

Many people have helped change the economy of North Carolina. Some people have worked to make businesses run better. Others have helped workers in North Carolina or started new businesses. **What might you learn about the ways people have affected North Carolina's economy?**

_____

_____

▷ **Many people work in downtown Charlotte, North Carolina.**

NORTH CAROLINA STANDARD COURSE OF STUDY

5.07 Identify historic figures and leaders who have influenced the economies of communities and evaluate the effectiveness of their contributions.

Furniture in North Carolina

In the early 1800s, Thomas Day was one of the best-known furniture makers in North Carolina. Day was a free African American who lived in Milton. His handmade cabinets and other furniture were very popular. By 1850, he owned the largest furniture business in the state. By 1861, Day had begun using steam-powered machines and mass production to add to the amount of furniture his business made. In **mass production**, many goods that are alike can be made quickly and cheaply using machines.

In 1881, brothers David and William White opened the White Furniture Company in Mebane. The White brothers used machines to make goods.

▶ People still admire Thomas Day's furniture today. Some of his furniture is still used. Other pieces are in museums.

▶ The White Furniture Company factory in Mebane, North Carolina

Eight years later, Ernest A. Snow started the High Point Furniture Company in High Point, North Carolina. High Point was a good place for making furniture because forests and sawmills were nearby.

Today, many people in North Carolina work in the furniture industry. They use computers to design furniture instead of drawing designs by hand. Then they use tools to cut the wood to the sizes and shapes needed. People from all over the United States buy furniture from North Carolina. In fact, the largest furniture factory in the United States is in High Point, North Carolina.

TextWork

4 Circle two reasons why High Point was a good place for making furniture.

5 Underline the way in which people in the furniture industry use computers.

6 Where is the largest furniture factory in the United States located?

_____

_____

▶ Ernest A. Snow (inset) started the High Point Furniture Company in High Point.

▶ A present-day woodworker makes chair legs.

▶ Employees of North Carolina Mutual Life Insurance Company—Susan V. Gille Norfleet, Charles Clinton Spaulding, and John Merrick (above). The North Carolina Mutual Life Insurance Company building (right).

Life Insurance in North Carolina

John Merrick, a former slave, wanted everyone to have a chance to get life insurance. People often buy life insurance so that when they die, their family will have enough money to live. By 1898, Merrick had started the North Carolina Mutual Life Insurance Company in Durham.

In 1899, Charles Clinton Spaulding began working at the life insurance company. In 1923, he became president of the company.

Spaulding helped North Carolina Mutual Life Insurance grow. At one time, the company had more than 1,000 employees. Today, it offers life insurance to people across the country.

TextWork

7 Who worked to bring life insurance to people in North Carolina and across the country?

_____

_____

8 Draw circles around the people pictured above who worked in life insurance in North Carolina.

Banking in North Carolina

During the 1980s, Hugh L. McColl worked to help North Carolina banks grow. He helped one North Carolina bank grow to serve seven surrounding states. In time, this bank became one of the largest banks in the United States.

In 1998, McColl helped join his bank with another large bank based in California to form the first nationwide bank. Today, nationwide banks serve communities around the country.

McColl's leadership helped make Charlotte the second-largest banking city in the United States. Today, the nation-wide bank he helped form, along with many of the country's largest banks, has its headquarters in Charlotte.

▶ The skyline of Charlotte, North Carolina

TextWork

9 How did Hugh L. McColl help North Carolina's economy?

_____

_____

_____

10 Circle the name of the North Carolina city in which several banking businesses have their headquarters today.

▶ Hugh L. McColl

TextWork

11 Underline three ways that women have helped the economy of North Carolina.

12 How did Martha McKay help women in businesses in North Carolina?

_____

_____

_____

_____

Women and the Economy

Many women have helped make the economy in North Carolina stronger. Some have worked to help women do well in the workplace. Others have started their own businesses.

Martha McKay

During the 1940s, Martha McKay studied economics at the University of North Carolina. In the early 1960s, she became active in the women's rights movement. This movement worked to get women equal rights. She worked to get equal pay for women in the workplace.

In 1976, McKay began the Women's Forum of North Carolina. This group worked to help women in their careers.

▶ **Martha McKay**

▶ **Darleen M. Johns**

The group taught women how to be good leaders in business and in government. Because of her work, more women became involved in North Carolina's businesses.

Darleen M. Johns

In 1979, Darleen M. Johns started her own company in the technology field. She was the first woman to own a technology company in the Raleigh area.

Today, Johns's company helps other businesses get and use the technology they need. Her company works toward improving the economy of her community and helping others do well in business. In 2005, she received the "NC Notable" award for her work in business and the community.

TextWork

13 Circle one way in which Darleen M. Johns helps businesses in her community.

14 Underline the organization that Jessica Govea helped Cesar Chavez build.

Children in History

Jessica Govea

Jessica Govea worked in the fields near her home in Kern County, California. Jessica, her parents, and most of the other workers were Mexican. They earned very little money and were treated poorly. When Jessica was only seven years old, she helped her father organize workers into a group that asked for changes. One member of the group was Cesar Chavez.

By the age of 17, Jessica was working full-time for Chavez. She organized marches and worked in a service center that helped farm families. The organization that she helped Chavez build is known today as the United Farm Workers of America. It helps workers across the United States.

1. SUMMARIZE How have people affected the economy of North Carolina?

_____

_____

_____

2. How did **mass production** change the furniture industry of North Carolina?

_____

_____

_____

3. Why do people buy life insurance?

_____

_____

_____

4. How did the White brothers and Ernest A. Snow change the furniture industry in North Carolina?

_____

_____

_____

MATCHING Draw a line connecting each person on the left with the North Carolina industry on the right that he or she helped shape.

5. Thomas Day   technology

6. Hugh L. McColl   furniture

7. Darleen M. Johns   banking

writing

✏ **Do Research** Research one of the people in this lesson. Write a paragraph about how that person helped change North Carolina's economy.

Review and Test Prep

 The Big Idea

People in a community depend on one another to make, buy, and sell goods and services.

Summarize the Unit

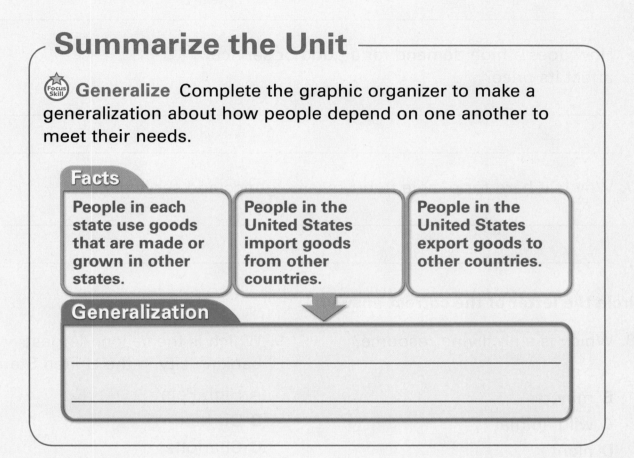

Focus Skill **Generalize** Complete the graphic organizer to make a generalization about how people depend on one another to meet their needs.

Facts

| People in each state use goods that are made or grown in other states. | People in the United States import goods from other countries. | People in the United States export goods to other countries. |

Generalization

_____

_____

Use Vocabulary

Draw a line connecting each term with its definition.

1. the making of goods in large quantities   **renewable,** p. 129

2. to do one kind of work   **interstate trade,** p. 134

3. able to be made a resource again   **specialize,** p. 140

4. buying and selling between states   **mass production,** p. 154

Think About It

5. Why are natural resources an important economic resource?

_____

_____

6. How does a high demand for a good or service affect its price?

_____

_____

7. Why is it hard for people to buy scarce goods and services?

_____

_____

Circle the letter of the correct answer.

8. Which is a nonliving resource?

  A tree

  B mineral

  C wild animal

  D plant

9. Which is the second-largest banking city in the United States?

  A High Point

  B Durham

  C Charlotte

  D Raleigh

Show What You Know

Writing **Write a Paragraph**
Explain how consumers affect what businesses sell. Use a business in your community as an example.

Activity **Draw a Picture**
Draw and label an object that was made in another country. Label your drawing to tell where the object was made.

GO online To play a game that reviews the unit, join Eco in the North Carolina Adventures online or on CD.

People and Technology

Spotlight on Goals and Objectives

North Carolina Interactive Presentations

NORTH CAROLINA STANDARD COURSE OF STUDY

COMPETENCY GOAL 6 The learner will recognize how technology is used at home, school, and in the community.

Research Triangle Park, North Carolina

💡 The Big Idea

How do people use technology at home, at school, and in the community?

Many tools people use today are different from the ones people used long ago. Think about what it would be like to read this book by candlelight or by the light of an oil lamp. Imagine trying to make a piece of toast without a toaster. Think about what it would be like not to have telephones or the Internet. Imagine what travel would be like without automobiles and airplanes.

Thanks to technology, people are able to do things more quickly and easily than in the past. Technology has changed the way people live by making people's lives easier at home, at school, and in the community.

Think about two tools you use every day at home, at school, and in your community. Then describe how these tools make your life easier.

Tools you use at home:

1. _____

2. _____

Tools you use at school:

1. _____

2. _____

Tools you use in your community:

1. _____

2. _____

Reading Social Studies

Categorize and Classify

❯ Learn

- When you **categorize** and **classify**, you sort things into groups.
- Decide what each group should be called. Place each thing in the group to which it belongs.

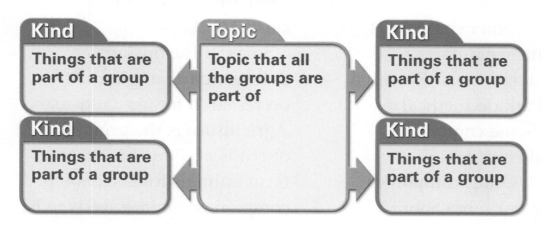

❯ Practice

Read the paragraph. Underline the category of art museums. Circle places that can be classified as art museums.

Research Triangle Park has many activities that people can do. People who enjoy playing sports can play softball or volleyball. People who enjoy outdoor activities can go canoeing, bicycling, and hiking. People who enjoy art museums can visit the Ackland Art Museum and the North Carolina Museum of Art. People can also visit history museums, such as the North Carolina Museum of History.

Categorize

Classify

Apply

Read the following paragraphs.

Research Triangle Park

Many businesses have their offices in Research Triangle Park. Many of these businesses work with technology. Some companies work with computers. Other companies work to make car parts.

Many companies at Research Triangle Park do medical research. Some companies make medicines and medical equipment. Other companies try to find out more about certain diseases.

Many groups at Research Triangle Park also work with the environment. One company works to protect forests in the southern United States. Another company works to keep water clean.

Some of the businesses at Research Triangle Park do research for agriculture. Agriculture is the growing of crops and the raising of farm animals for sale. Some companies prepare seeds to be planted. Other companies work on ways to protect crops.

Use the graphic organizer below to categorize and classify the types of work done at Research Triangle Park.

Technology

computers
_____
_____

Topic

Businesses located in Research Triangle Park

Medical

_____
_____
_____

Environment

_____
_____
_____

Agriculture

_____
_____

Leaders in Technology

Over time, many people have made contributions to technology. **Technology** is all of the tools that people use in everyday life. Leaders in technology have thought of ways to make new goods called **inventions**. Many inventions help make people's lives easier. People who make inventions are called **inventors**. **What will you learn about leaders in technology?**

_____

_____

» **The National Inventors Hall of Fame, Akron, Ohio**

NORTH CAROLINA STANDARD COURSE OF STUDY

6.02 Identify and describe contributions made by community leaders in technology.

Inventors in Communication

Long ago, people did not have many ways to **communicate**, or to share information, with others who were far away. In the 1800s and the 1900s, new inventions made communicating faster and easier.

In 1840, Samuel Morse invented the telegraph. This machine used a code of dots and dashes to send messages over wires. Before long, telegraph wires crossed the country. People could get news quickly from faraway places.

Alexander Graham Bell also changed the way people communicated. In 1877, he started the first telephone company. For the first time, people could speak to and hear from others who were far away.

❶ When was the telegraph invented?

_____

❷ In the pictures below, circle the person who started the first telephone company.

➤ Samuel Morse invented the telegraph (left).

➤ Alexander Graham Bell was the first person to start telephone service.

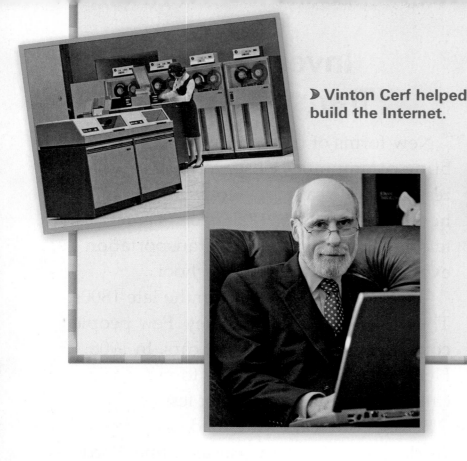

▶ Vinton Cerf helped build the Internet.

▶ Ray Tomlinson found a way to send electronic messages over the Internet.

In the late 1960s, computers at several California universities were connected by wires to "talk" to one another. One student who worked on this project was Vinton Cerf. He helped build a system that links computers around the world. Today, the system is known as the **Internet**.

Ray Tomlinson, an engineer in Massachusetts, found a way to use the Internet to send electronic messages. These electronic messages are called **e-mail**. It was his idea to use the symbol @ (at) in electronic message addresses. He said, "I thought about other symbols, but [@] didn't appear in any names, so it worked."

✏️ **TextWork**

❸ What system did Vinton Cerf help create?

_____

❹ Which inventor found a way to send electronic messages over the Internet?

_____

❺ Circle the symbol in the pictures above used in electronic messages.

TextWork

6 Underline the text that describes the term *assembly line.*

7 How did the assembly line help the production of cars?

_____

_____

_____

Henry Ford's Model T was the first car in the United States that many people could afford to buy.

Inventors in Transportation

New forms of transportation helped bring communities closer together. As a result, people can now work farther from home. They can also visit friends and family who live far away. Transportation even helps students get to school.

Cars were first invented in the late 1800s. These cars cost a lot of money. Few people could afford to buy the first cars. In 1908, Henry Ford invented a way to make a car, called the Model T, that cost less.

Before Ford, cars were made by a few workers who built one car at a time. Ford divided the jobs among many workers along an assembly line. On an **assembly line**, each worker adds one kind of part to a product as it passes on a moving belt.

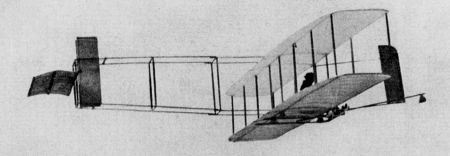

Wilbur and Orville Wright built an airplane that could fly.

Ford's assembly line allowed Model Ts to be assembled, or put together, faster and at a lower cost. Ford's assembly line also made it possible to make a large number of cars at the same time. More people could afford them, and cars became the main form of transportation.

In 1903, Orville Wright made the first airplane flight at Kitty Hawk, North Carolina. It lasted for 12 seconds. Orville and his brother, Wilbur, had built the airplane. They had been building and improving airplanes for several years. Later, airplane companies used the Wright brothers' ideas to build larger airplanes. Today, airplanes carry both people and goods around the world.

TextWork

8 Where did Orville Wright make his first airplane flight?

_____

9 List three inventors who changed transportation.

_____

_____

_____

▶Thomas Edison (left) and Lewis Latimer (right) invented the first practical light bulb.

▶An old electric lightbulb

 TextWork

Inventions Used in Homes and Schools

Lightbulbs, computers, and televisions are all inventions that are used in homes and schools. These inventions have changed the way people live.

Many inventors worked together to bring electricity to homes and schools. In the 1880s, Thomas Edison and Lewis Latimer invented the first practical electric lightbulb. Before the lightbulb, people used candles and gas and oil lamps for light.

The lightbulb let people light homes and schools without the danger of causing a fire. The lightbulb also let people do more evening activities. Electric lighting let people work more hours, which let them get more work done in a day.

Today, computers are found in many homes and schools around the world. In 1964, Donald L. Bitzer helped invent the flat plasma screen. This screen is easier to look at than other types of computer screens. It was invented to help students who had to work in front of computers for long periods of time.

Bitzer's invention has also improved televisions, which were first invented in the early 1900s. Many newer televisions are being made with the flat plasma screen technology.

TextWork

12 What did Donald L. Bitzer help invent?

_____

13 Which two types of technology did Donald L. Bitzer's invention improve?

_____

_____

▶ Donald L. Bitzer was given an award for improving television technology.

1. **SUMMARIZE** How have inventors made contributions to technology?

_____

_____

_____

_____

2. Write a sentence that describes the word **inventions**.

_____

_____

_____

3. List three inventors who changed the ways in which people communicate.

_____

_____

_____

4. How would your life be different if the Internet had not been invented?

_____

_____

_____

_____

MATCHING Draw a line connecting each inventor on the left with the correct invention on the right.

5. Henry Ford   telegraph

6. Samuel Morse   practical lightbulb

7. Thomas Edison and Lewis Latimer   assembly line

 Make a Chart Make a chart of inventors and their inventions.

Technology has changed the ways people around the world live and work. Technology has changed the ways people communicate. It has also changed the kinds of transportation people use. **What do you think you will learn about how technology has affected communities?**

_____

_____

Technology workers checking a computer system

NORTH CAROLINA STANDARD COURSE OF STUDY

6.03 Identify the impact of technological change on communities around the world.

 **TextWork**

① Underline four examples listed in the text of ways people communicate.

② Circle examples shown in the pictures below of ways in which people communicate.

Changes in Communication

Technology has changed the way people in different communities around the world communicate. When telephones were first invented, people used them only to talk. Today, people also use telephone lines to send written and visual information. Fax machines deliver information on paper over telephone lines. People use cell phones to talk and to send pictures, music, and written messages.

▶ **People can use cell phones to communicate from most places on Earth.**

Around the world, people use the Internet to get information and to talk to other people. The Internet has made communicating faster and easier.

At home, the Internet can help people keep in touch with friends and family. At school, some students can e-mail their teachers about homework. People can also use the Internet at work. At work, people can use the Internet to hold video business meetings with people in communities that are far away.

TextWork

❸ List three places in which people can use the Internet for communication.

_____

_____

_____

➤ An Internet cafe provides Internet service for a fee.

 **TextWork**

4 List five examples of technology which have helped connect communities.

_____

_____

_____

_____

_____

Changes in Transportation

Technology has helped communities grow. Roads, canals, cars, railroads, and airplanes have helped connect communities around the world.

When railroads were first built, they brought change to communities. People used railroads to move things to markets. As a result, new businesses opened. New communities were started. Communities located along the railroads grew larger. The communities became connected because it was easy to travel between them by train.

In the early 1900s, cars became the main form of transportation. People could live outside cities and drive to work. Cars led to the building of highways across the country.

▶ Cars and trains help people travel to and from nearby cities.

▶ Today, people can fly to places across the United States and around the world.

▶ In the future, a rail system will connect the North Carolina cities of Durham, Cary, and Raleigh.

Most families today have cars that they use to drive to work or school. Larger cities around the world have public transportation. **Public transportation** moves large numbers of people from place to place. Buses, subways, and trains are types of public transportation.

Public transportation helps the world's communities conserve, or save, energy. It also helps them reduce pollution and traffic. Cities such as New York City, London, and Tokyo have large public rail systems. Charlotte was the first North Carolina city to have a rail system.

 TextWork

5 Name one example of public transportation shown in the pictures on pages 178–179.

_____

6 Name the first North Carolina city to have a rail system.

_____

TextWork

7 In the text, underline the three cities that are connected by Research Triangle.

8 LOCATION On the map, circle the universities that are located at the Research Triangle's three points.

Research Triangle Park

Map Key
- University
- Research Triangle
- Research Triangle Park

Changes in North Carolina

In the 1950s, Governor Luther Hodges wanted to bring jobs in technology to North Carolina. A group of leaders worked to set up a place where several companies could be built near one another. As a result, Research Triangle Park was set up in 1959.

Research Triangle Park is about 8 miles long and 2 miles wide. It is in an imaginary triangle connecting Chapel Hill, Durham, and Raleigh. At the points of the triangle are the University of North Carolina, North Carolina State University, and Duke University.

❯ Former governor of North Carolina, Luther Hodges, reviewing plans for Research Triangle Park

▶ This man demonstrates a dry-cleaning unit made at Research Triangle Park.

About 145 organizations are located in Research Triangle Park. Many of these are technology companies, such as IBM and Sony Ericsson. These companies research ways to improve technology. Other companies research medicine and the environment.

Today, almost 40,000 people work at Research Triangle Park. In fact, it is one of the largest research parks in the world. Research Triangle Park has helped the cities of Chapel Hill, Durham, and Raleigh grow. Today, about 1.5 million people live in the Research Triangle Park area.

▶ Doctors at Research Triangle Park develop medicines to treat diseases.

1. **SUMMARIZE** How has technology affected communities around the world?

_____

_____

_____

2. How does **public transportation** help communities around the world?

_____

_____

3. List three ways in which people communicate today.

_____

_____

_____

4. How did people's lives change after cars became the main form of transportation in the United States?

_____

_____

_____

_____

5. Why was Research Triangle Park created?

_____

_____

_____

_____

writing

✎ **Write a Paragraph** Write a paragraph that describes ways in which technology has changed your community.

Technology and the Economy

Lesson

3

Technology has affected the economy in a number of ways. It has changed the ways people do business and the ways people buy and sell goods. Technology has also changed the ways in which people move goods between communities. **What will you learn about technology and the economy?**

_____

_____

▶ A port on the Cape Fear River, Wilmington, North Carolina

**NORTH CAROLINA
STANDARD COURSE OF STUDY**

6.01 Describe and assess ways in which technology is used in a community's economy.

Unit 6 ■ 183

TextWork

❶ Underline the definition of the term *communication link* in the text.

❷ Study the flowchart below. Circle the steps shown that use computers.

Electronic Buying and Selling

Communication links have changed the way people buy and sell goods. A **communication link** is something that lets people who are far apart share information instantly. In the past, people had to meet face to face to buy and sell goods. Today, many businesses sell goods and services through the Internet. Buying and selling in this way is often called e-commerce. *Commerce* means "business." **E-commerce** lets people buy and sell goods and services through the Internet.

Online Buying and Selling

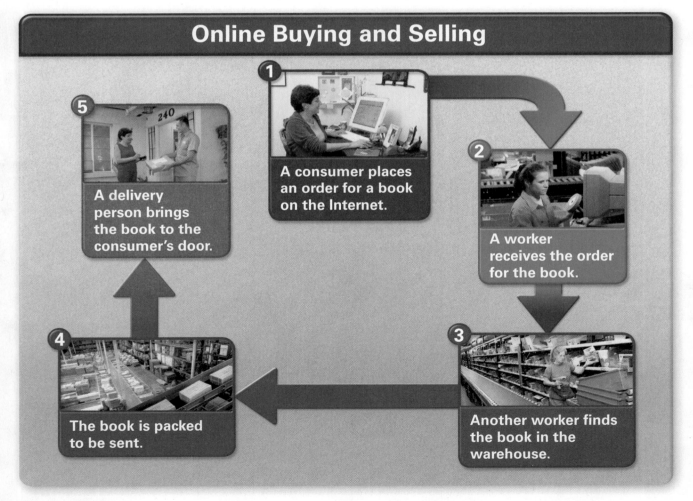

1. A consumer places an order for a book on the Internet.

2. A worker receives the order for the book.

3. Another worker finds the book in the warehouse.

4. The book is packed to be sent.

5. A delivery person brings the book to the consumer's door.

Telephones and fax machines are also used to buy and sell goods and services. People can place orders over the phone or by fax from catalogs. Catalogs provide pictures and information about goods.

Consumers can choose to pay for goods and services with debit cards or credit cards. Information from the card is sent through a communication link to a bank.

Internet Advertisements

Many businesses place advertisements about their goods and services on the Internet. An **advertisement** is a notice made to get people to buy something. People from communities around the world can see advertisments. They can order what they want from any computer that is connected to the Internet.

> A consumer orders goods through the Internet.

 **TextWork**

❸ List the words in the advertisement that might make people more interested in the helmet being advertised.

_____

_____

_____

THE "GLOBE-PRO" BICYCLE HELMET

THE ULTIMATE IN HEAD GEAR!

WEAR THE COOLEST HELMET ON THE BLOCK!

ALL OF YOUR FRIENDS WILL WANT ONE!

COMES IN A VARIETY OF COLORS

> An advertisement

Moving Goods

4 How has modern transportation changed the amount of time it takes for goods to be shipped?

_____

_____

_____

5 What two types of transportation used to move goods are shown below?

_____

_____

_____

6 How did McLean's invention change the way goods were transported?

_____

_____

_____

Communities around the world often have to trade to get the goods they need. How are heavy logs moved from Canada to the United States? How does oil from Venezuela get to France? How do fish from North Carolina reach other states without spoiling?

Changes in **modern**, or present-day, transportation make international trade possible. Trains, ships, and airplanes move goods to and from communities faster than ever. Keeping foods cool allows them to be moved over long distances.

❯ Goods travel across the United States by airplanes and by trains.

With modern transportation, goods arrive in days or weeks instead of in months or years. Canada's logs travel on trucks and trains to cities in the United States that need them. Oil travels across oceans in large ships. Fish are packed in ice and flown on refrigerated airplanes to many places.

❯ A truck carries logs along an interstate highway.

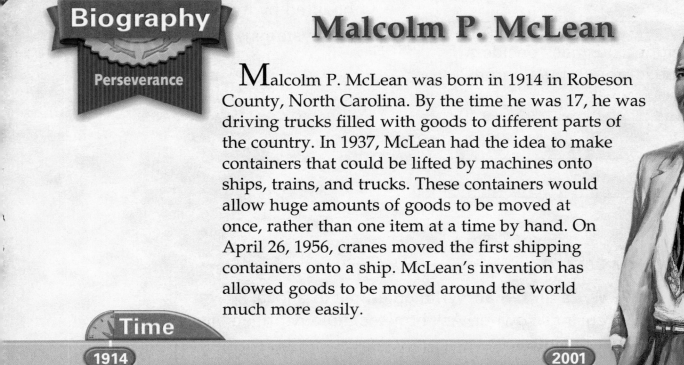

Biography

Perseverance

Malcolm P. McLean

Malcolm P. McLean was born in 1914 in Robeson County, North Carolina. By the time he was 17, he was driving trucks filled with goods to different parts of the country. In 1937, McLean had the idea to make containers that could be lifted by machines onto ships, trains, and trucks. These containers would allow huge amounts of goods to be moved at once, rather than one item at a time by hand. On April 26, 1956, cranes moved the first shipping containers onto a ship. McLean's invention has allowed goods to be moved around the world much more easily.

Time

1914	2001
Born	Died

● **1956** First shipping containers loaded onto a ship

1. **SUMMARIZE** How has technology changed the economies of communities?

_____

_____

_____

_____

2. How does a **communication link** affect a business?

_____

_____

3. Why might a business decide to sell goods through the Internet?

_____

_____

_____

4. What are some ways to transport goods from one place to another?

_____

_____

_____

Circle the letter of the correct answer.

5. What did Malcolm P. McLean invent?

   A telegraph

   B e-commerce

   C shipping containers that could be lifted by machines

   D rail systems

writing

Write an E-mail Write an e-mail to a local business owner. Ask how technology affects his or her business.

Review and Test Prep

💡 **The Big Idea**

People use technology at home, at school, and in the community.

Summarize the Unit

⭐ **Categorize and Classify** Complete the graphic organizer to categorize and classify what you learned about the ways in which people use technology.

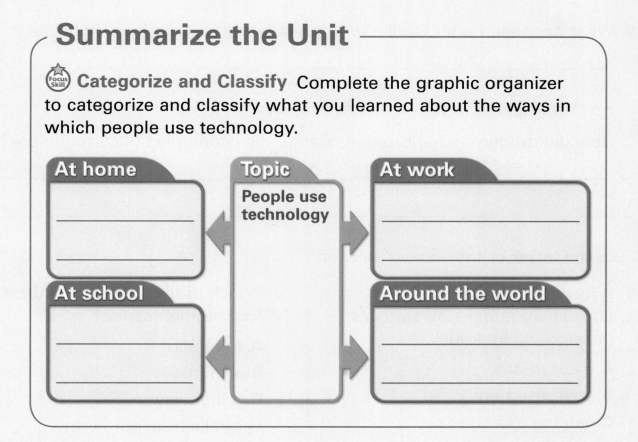

At home

_____

_____

Topic

People use technology

At work

_____

_____

At school

_____

_____

Around the world

_____

_____

Use Vocabulary

Draw a line connecting each term with its definition.

1. ways of moving large numbers of people from place to place

2. all of the tools that people use in everyday life

3. people who make something new for the first time

4. how we describe the time we live in today

technology, p. 167

inventors, p. 167

public transportation, p. 179

modern, p. 186

5. How did Alexander Graham Bell change the way people communicated?

_____

_____

6. What happened after Orville Wright made the first airplane flight?

_____

_____

7. How did modern transportation change the economies of communities?

_____

_____

Circle the letter of the correct answer.

8. Which best descibes buying and selling goods and services through the Internet?

   A e-commerce

   B advertisement

   C catalog

   D e-mail

9. Which of the following is used for communication?

   A the Internet

   B a railroad

   C a highway

   D public transportation

Show What You Know

Writing Write a Thank-You Note
Write a thank-you note to an inventor or another person whose work has changed people's lives.

Activity Make an Advertisement
Make an advertisement for one kind of technology you use. Include reasons that this is a good item to buy.

GO online To play a game that reviews the unit, join Eco in the North Carolina Adventures online or on CD.

People Shape Communities

A storyteller at the Catawba Storytelling Festival in Catawba County, North Carolina

Spotlight on Goals and Objectives

North Carolina Interactive Presentations

NORTH CAROLINA STANDARD COURSE OF STUDY

COMPETENCY GOAL 7 The learner will analyze the role of real and fictional heroes in shaping the culture of communities.

ECO

The Big Idea

How do real and fictional people help shape the
culture of a community?

Every person can make a difference in his or her
community. Some people become leaders to help others.
Others work with their neighbors to make the area in which
they live better. Many of these people are heroes in their
communities.

Heroes make a difference in people's lives with their
words, actions, and discoveries. They take action, and they
stand up for what they believe. Heroes often help shape the
culture of an area because they set an example for other
people living in the community.

Some everyday heroes in your community may be
parents, firefighters, police officers, or volunteers. Other
people sometimes become heroes based on made-up
stories about them. All heroes make a difference in people's
lives by making communities better places in which to live.

**Think of a hero in your life. Describe your hero in a
paragraph. Tell why this person is a hero and how this
person makes your life better.**

_____

_____

_____

_____

_____

Reading Social Studies

 ## Cause and Effect

❱ Learn

A **cause** is something that makes something else happen. An **effect** is what happens as a result.

- Words and phrases such as *because, as a result, since,* and *so* can help you identify why something happens.
- An effect can also become a cause for another event.

Cause	Effect
An event or action	What happens

❱ Practice

Underline one effect of stories being passed down from generation to generation.

Today, people watch television or listen to the radio for fun. When settlers first came to North Carolina, they did not have these kinds of technology. As a result, families would often gather to tell stories for fun. Stories were often passed down from generation to generation, so some of them have been around for a long time.

Cause

Effect

> **Apply**

Read the following paragraphs.

Storytelling—A Part of North Carolina's History

European settlers brought many stories with them to North Carolina. African Americans and American Indians also brought stories to North Carolina. As a result, North Carolina's stories come from many different cultures.

Storytelling is an important part of North Carolina's history. It is often used to teach people about history and heroes.

Mecklenburg County holds a Storytelling Festival each November. People from across the state come to celebrate the tradition of storytelling. At the festival, puppet shows and music are used to tell well-known stories. People can take classes to improve their storytelling skills.

Complete the chart below.

Cause		Effect
_____ _____ _____ _____	→	Many of North Carolina's stories come from different cultures.
Storytelling is an important part of North Carolina's history.	→	_____ _____ _____

Local and Global Leaders

Many people show that they care about their community by being heroes. A **hero** is a person who does something important and sets an example for others. Local leaders in the United States work to make a difference in their cities, states, or country. Global leaders work to make a difference in countries around the world. **What will you learn about local and global leaders?**

_____

_____

▶ **The United Nations Building in New York City, New York**

NORTH CAROLINA STANDARD COURSE OF STUDY

7.01 Identify the deeds of local and global leaders.

❶ Why was Rosa Parks arrested?

_____

_____

❷ What happened as a result of Parks's arrest?

_____

_____

_____

▶ Rosa Parks worked for justice (inset). The bus on which she refused to give up her seat is now in a museum (right).

Local Leaders

Local leaders work to make their communities better places to live. Many times, their work helps people in other communities, too.

Rosa Parks

Rosa Parks wanted to change laws that were unfair to African Americans. In some places in the 1950s, African Americans had to sit in the back of public buses. They could sit in the middle only if white people did not need the seats.

In 1955, Parks was sitting in a middle seat of a bus in Montgomery, Alabama. The bus filled up. When she refused to give up her seat, she was arrested. After Parks was arrested, many people refused to ride any bus in Montgomery. As a result, the bus company lost money. After almost a year, the law was changed to allow African Americans to sit anywhere on a bus.

People from all over the world visit the house of Levi Coffin in Newport, Indiana (below).

Dolores Huerta worked with Cesar Chavez to form the National Farm Workers Association.

LEVI COFFIN

Levi Coffin (1798-1877), a Quaker abolitionist, lived in Newport (now Fountain City) with his family 1826-1847. Moved from North Carolina because he and his wife, Catharine, opposed slavery. Advocated, and sold in his store, free-labor products not produced by slaves. House built circa 1839; designated a National Historic Landmark 1966.

Dolores Huerta

Because many farmworkers were not United States citizens, they did not have many rights. Dolores Huerta taught the workers how to become citizens and how to vote. Later, she helped them find more ways to earn money.

Levi Coffin

Levi Coffin was born in New Garden, North Carolina. In 1826, he moved to Newport, Indiana. Newport was a stop on the Underground Railroad. The **Underground Railroad** was not a real railroad but a series of routes and houses used by escaped slaves on their journey north to freedom. Coffin helped about 3,000 escaped slaves find freedom. Today, Coffin is remembered by some as the president of the Underground Railroad.

TextWork

❸ Circle the text that tells why many farmworkers did not have many rights.

❹ Underline the text that explains how Dolores Huerta helped farmworkers in the United States.

❺ Whom did Levi Coffin help as part of the Underground Railroad?

_____

_____

Global Leaders

Global leaders work to make changes for people around the world. These leaders work to help people in other communities.

Mohandas Gandhi

For years, India had been ruled by Britain. Many people in India were treated unfairly and unequally. Mohandas Gandhi (moh•HAHN•dahs GAHN•dee) wanted people in India to have freedom. Instead of fighting, he used peaceful actions to work for equality. He led marches and refused to follow laws that he felt were wrong.

In 1947, India won its independence from Britain. Gandhi had helped the people of India become free.

▶ A statue of Mohandas Gandhi

▶ Mohandas Gandhi was a leader for equality in India.

▶ In 2002, Jimmy Carter was awarded the Nobel Peace Prize for his work.

Jimmy Carter

Jimmy Carter served as President of the United States from 1977 to 1981. Today, he works for peace in countries around the world. He helps nations that disagree solve their problems peacefully. He also volunteers for Habitat for Humanity.

Wangari Maathai

Wangari Maathai (wan•GAH•ree mah•TY) was the first woman in eastern and central Africa to earn a doctoral degree. In Kenya, Africa, Maathai started a group called the Green Belt Movement. This group has planted 30 million trees to help keep Kenya's soil from turning into desert. People in other countries have borrowed Maathai's idea of planting trees. In 2004, Maathai won the Nobel Peace Prize for her work.

TextWork

6 How did Mohandas Gandhi work for equality?

_____

_____

7 For which group does Jimmy Carter volunteer?

_____

_____

8 Underline the text that describes what the Green Belt Movement has done in Kenya.

▶ Jimmy Carter and his wife, Rosalynn, help build homes for Habitat for Humanity.

▶ Wangari Maathai was the first African woman to win the Nobel Peace Prize.

1. **SUMMARIZE** How have local and global leaders helped their communities?

_____

_____

_____

2. Write a short description of the word **hero**.

_____

_____

_____

3. How did Rosa Parks help her community?

_____

_____

_____

4. How did Mohandas Gandhi work for change?

_____

_____

_____

_____

5. What was one effect of the Green Belt Movement?

_____

_____

_____

_____

writing

✏️ **Write a Newspaper Article** Choose a leader who has made a difference in North Carolina, the United States, or the world. Research this person. Use the facts you find to write a short article, and add it to a class newspaper.

People express their culture in many ways. One way to express culture is through stories. Many stories are about characters who do heroic deeds. **What might you learn about the heroes of stories?**

_____

_____

▶ **An American Indian telling a story at a festival**

**NORTH CAROLINA
STANDARD COURSE OF STUDY**

7.02 Assess the heroic deeds of characters from folktales and legends.

Folktales

A **folktale** is a story passed from one generation to the next. Folktales help keep alive the traditions of a culture. Folktales can tell about a culture's people, the places where they live, and their beliefs.

Jacktales

Jacktales are folktales from Europe that were shared by and added to by people who settled in the Appalachian Mountains. In most of the Jacktales, a boy named Jack meets challenges and becomes a hero.

Paul Bunyan

One American tall tale hero is Paul Bunyan. A **tall tale** uses humorous exaggeration to explain how something came to be. Paul Bunyan is a make-believe giant with great strength.

❶ Circle three things that a folktale can tell about a culture.

❷ From which continent are the Jacktales?

_____

❸ Underline the text that describes a *tall tale*.

▶ **Many stories about Paul Bunyan include his great blue ox, Babe.**

In one story, he digs a hole in the ground that becomes Puget Sound, a body of water in Washington state. In another story, he clears trees to get the land ready for settlers.

Pecos Bill

Pecos Bill is a tall tale hero known for his strength, courage, and humor. Edward O'Reilly wrote the first stories about Pecos Bill in 1923. O'Reilly claimed that the stories came from real tales told by cowhands.

Stories tell that Pecos Bill was born in Texas in the 1830s. After falling out of his parents' covered wagon near the Pecos River, he was raised by coyotes. One dry year, he drained the Rio Grande to water his ranch—the entire state of New Mexico!

TextWork

4 Who wrote the first Pecos Bill stories?

_____

_____

5 Circle the text that describes why Pecos Bill drained the Rio Grande.

❯ Pecos Bill rode a mountain lion and used a rattlesnake as a whip.

Legends

Many people also share legends from their cultures. A **legend** is a made-up story about a real person or event.

❻ What is a *legend*?

_____

_____

_____

❼ Why was John Chapman nicknamed Johnny Appleseed?

_____

_____

_____

❽ Underline the text that describes what caused Mary Slocumb to search for her husband during the American Revolution.

Johnny Appleseed

One American legend is based on John Chapman, an American pioneer born in Massachusetts. For more than 40 years, he traveled around Ohio, Indiana, and Illinois, selling or giving away apple seeds to people he met along the way. He helped hundreds of settlers set up apple orchards. During his life, Chapman became a symbol of the pioneer spirit in the United States. He was given the nickname Johnny Appleseed. Legend has it that the apple trees of the Ohio River valley bloom with apple blossoms each spring thanks to Johnny Appleseed.

❯ John Chapman became a symbol of the pioneer spirit in the United States

Daniel Boone

The story of Daniel Boone is another American legend. Boone helped open the West to settlement by clearing a path through the Appalachian Mountains. The stories of his brave deeds and daring adventures made him a national hero.

Mary Slocumb

During the American Revolution, Mary Slocumb became a North Carolina legend. The story goes that in 1776, while Slocumb's husband was off at war, she had a dream that he was in danger. When she woke up, she got on her horse and rode 60 miles, stopping where she heard the sounds of battle. At the battleground, she searched for her husband but found many wounded men instead. She cleaned and bandaged their wounds. Hours later, Slocumb's husband appeared. He had not been injured.

❯ This powder horn (above) was used by Daniel Boone (inset).

❯ The legend of Mary Slocumb tells of how she saved the lives of many North Carolinians one night.

1. **SUMMARIZE** How do folktales and legends help people learn about the heroic deeds of people?

_____

_____

_____

_____

2. How is a **folktale** different from a **tall tale**?

_____

_____

_____

3. What kinds of qualities do you think many Americans admire?

_____

_____

_____

4. How is a legend related to real life?

_____

_____

_____

_____

Circle the letter of the correct answer.

5. During which war did Mary Slocumb become a North Carolina legend?

   A French Revolution

   B War of 1812

   C American Revolution

   D Civil War

writing

✎ **Write a Folktale** Choose a physical feature in your community. Write a folktale that explains how it got there.

Creating New Communities

In some stories, **fictional**, or made-up, people help create new communities. In the fictional story *Where I Live* by Pleasant DeSpain, Hunter Bickford tells about his experience immigrating to America with his mother. There they helped start the community of Fort Read, North Carolina. **What do you think you will learn from the story of the fictional people in this lesson?**

_____

_____

Hunter Bickford and his mother

**NORTH CAROLINA
STANDARD COURSE OF STUDY**

7.03 Explore the role of selected fictional characters in creating new communities.

❶ Who wrote to Hunter's mother to get her to move to North Carolina?

_____

❷ Underline the text that describes why Hunter and his mother came to the Americas.

▶ **Uncle Edwin wrote about the opportunities in North Carolina (inset), so Hunter and his mother made the journey across the Atlantic Ocean (below).**

WHERE I LIVE
by Pleasant DeSpain

My name is Hunter Bickford, and this is the story of how I came to live in North Carolina.

Ma and I crossed the vast ocean to the Americas on a ship when I was nine. I remember the salty smell of the sea air. Pa had been a lieutenant in the British navy. He was killed when I was seven. I miss him still.

My Uncle Edwin, Ma's brother, had settled in New Bern, North Carolina, the year before we arrived. He wrote to Ma saying the area was good for farming and full of opportunities.

▶ **The people at the fort greeted Hunter and his mother.**

Ma is a good teacher. She taught me how to read, to write, and to do arithmetic. We came to the Americas so that Ma could find a job as a teacher. New Bern already had two teachers when we arrived, so Ma hired a boat to take us farther west.

We traveled 10 miles up the Neuse River and stopped at an old fort. It was built 60 years ago when the colonists were fighting with American Indians who lived nearby. Nine families were living in the fort when we arrived. I counted 13 children at the fort, too.

The general store, meeting hall, and church were in fort buildings. Men were building a large boat landing and dock. The fresh-cut wood smelled sweet.

 **TextWork**

❸ Why did Hunter and his mother leave New Bern?

_____

_____

_____

❹ Underline the text that describes when the fort was built.

TextWork

5 Circle the text that tells why Hunter and his mother stayed at the fort.

6 How many nights a week did the adults come to school?

_____

▶ Hunter helped build a cabin (inset) while his mother taught at the schoolhouse (below).

At the fort, I heard many different languages being spoken. Ma said the people living at the fort were from Germany, Scotland, and Sweden. She told me, "They need an English teacher, Hunter." So we decided to stay. An empty fort building became the new schoolhouse.

Three years have passed since we first arrived at the fort. There are now two big barns, a water-powered sawmill, and another church.

Three German men helped us build a log cabin. Slow-burning logs in our fireplace keep us warm on cold nights. The whine of the mill's blade cutting logs wakes us every morning.

The adults come to school two nights a week. Ma teaches them how to read, write, and speak English. A Swedish family arrived yesterday. The father asked, "Is this the place with the good teacher?"

▶ **Hunter's mother taught people in the community how to read and came up with the idea to name the community Fort Read.**

The forest is my second home. It is full of wild turkeys, fat rabbits, and swift deer. My friend Ben and I hunt and fish every day. My skinny dog named Bones goes with us.

Ma sews new buckskin clothes for me each year. She says if I grow any faster, I'll have to wear tree bark!

Our community has grown. There are now 32 families living here. There are 64 children! Ben's pa carved a new name above the old fort gate last month. *FORT READ*. It was Ma's idea.

TextWork

❼ Underline the number of families living at the fort.

❽ Circle the new name of the community.

1. **SUMMARIZE** How did the characters in this lesson help create a community?

_____

_____

_____

2. What does **fictional** mean?

_____

_____

_____

3. Why do you think that Hunter Bickford's mother chose the name Fort Read for the community?

_____

_____

_____

Circle the letter of the correct answer.

4. In which community did Hunter Bickford and his mother first arrive?

   A New Bern

   B Fort Read

   C Britain

   D Neuse River

5. What does Hunter say is his second home?

   A the fort

   B the sawmill

   C the forest

   D the general store

activity

Make a Poster Do research to find out how your community started. Present what you have learned on a poster about your community.

Review and Test Prep

 **The Big Idea**

Real and fictional people help shape the culture of communities.

Summarize the Unit

Cause and Effect Complete the graphic organizer to show that you understand the causes and effects of people shaping culture.

Cause

| Local leaders work to make a difference in their communities. |

Effect

| _____ _____ |

| _____ _____ |

| As a result, people in India became free, and about 30 million trees were planted in Kenya. |

Use Vocabulary

Draw a line connecting each term with its definition.

1. routes used by escaped slaves   **hero,** p. 195

2. sets an example for others   **Underground Railroad,** p. 197

3. a story that is passed from one   **folktale,** p. 202
   generation to the next

4. made-up   **fictional,** p. 207

Think About It

5. How did Rosa Parks work for change in the United States?

_____

_____

6. How did Dolores Huerta help farmworkers in the United States?

_____

_____

7. What are Jacktales?

_____

_____

Circle the letter of the correct answer.

8. Which of the following is a North Carolina legend?

   A Paul Bunyan

   B Pecos Bill

   C Mary Slocumb

   D Johnny Appleseed

9. What was the name of the community that Hunter Bickford and his mother helped start?

   A New Bern

   B Fort Read

   C Roanoke

   D Cumberland Gap

Show What You Know

Writing Write a Story
Write a fictional story about how a character helped shape the culture of your community.

Activity Create a Bulletin Board
Make a bulletin board about North Carolina legends. Draw and cut out pictures to illustrate the legends.

Go online To play a game that reviews the unit, join Eco in North Carolina Adventures online or on CD.

For Your Reference

GLOSSARY

INDEX

Glossary

The Glossary contains important history and social science words and their definitions, listed in alphabetical order. Each word is respelled as it would be in a dictionary. When you see this mark ' after a syllable, pronounce that syllable with more force. The page number at the end of the definition tells where the word is first defined in this book. Guide words at the top of each page help you quickly locate the word you need to find.

add, āce, câre, pälm; end, ēqual; it, īce; odd, ōpen, ôrder; to͝ok, po͞ol; up, bûrn; yo͞o as *u* in *fuse*; oil; pout; ə as *a* in *above*, *e* in *sicken*, *i* in *possible*, *o* in *melon*, *u* in *circus*; check; ring; thin; this; zh as in *vision*

A

absolute location (ab'sə•lo͞ot lō•kā'shən) The exact location of a place. p. 102

adapt (ə•dapt') To change. p. 113

advertisement (ad'vər•tīz•mənt) A notice made to get people to buy something. p. 185

amendment (ə•mend'mənt) A change to something that is already written. p. 81

ancient (ān'shənt) Happening or existing very long ago. p. 49

appoint (ə•point') To name. p. 19

assembly line (ə•sem'blē līn) A process for making goods in which each worker adds one part as a product passes on a moving belt. p. 170

B

ballot (ba'lət) A list of the choices in an election. p. 14

border (bôr'dər) On a map, a line that shows where a state or a nation ends. p. 94

C

canal (kə•nal') A human-made waterway dug across land. p. 119

candidate (kan'də•dāt) A person who wants to be elected as a leader. p. 14

capital resource (kap'ə•təl rē'sôrs) A tool or building a business needs to make and deliver a product. p. 131

cardinal directions (kär'də•nel di•rek'shənz) The main directions *north, south, east,* and *west.* p. I7

civil rights (si'vəl rīts) Rights that give everyone equal treatment. p. 32

climate (klī'mət) Weather that a place has over a long period of time. p. 105

colony (käl'ə•nē) A settlement that is ruled by another country. p. 84

common good (kä'mən go͝od) The good of everyone in a community. p. 6

communicate (kə•myo͞o'nə•kāt) To share information. p. 168

communication link (kə•myo͞o•nə•kā'shən lingk) A kind of technology that lets people who are far apart share information instantly. p. 184

compass rose (kum'pəs rōz) A drawing on a map that shows the cardinal directions to help people use the map. p. I7

consequence (kän'sə•kwens) Something that happens because of what a person does. p. 13

constitution (kän•stə•to͞o'shən) A written set of laws that describes how a government will work. p. 31

consumption (kən•səmp'shen) The using of goods to meet wants and needs. p. 151

continent (kän'tən•ənt) One of the seven largest land areas on Earth. p. I4

cooperative (kō•ä'pə•rə•tiv) A group of workers who own a business together. p. 144

culture (kul'chər) A way of life shared by members of a group. p. 29

D

dam (dam) A structure that is built to hold back water. p. 109

demand (di•mand') A willingness of consumers to buy goods and services. p. 137

distribution (dis•trə•byo͞o'shən) The sending of goods to stores to sell to conumers. p. 150

division of labor (də•vi'zhən uv lā'bər) The division of jobs among workers. p. 139

E

e-commerce (ē•kä′mərs) Buying and selling goods and services on the Internet. p. 184

economic resource (e•kə•nä′mik rē′sôrs) An available source or supply based on the production, distribution, and consumption of a good or service. p. 127

economy (i•kä′nə•mē) The ways a country or community makes and uses goods and services. p. 44

election (i•lek′shən) A time set aside for voting. p. 14

e-mail (ē′māl) An electronic message. p. 169

equator (i•kwā′tər) On a map or globe, a line that appears halfway between the North Pole and the South Pole. p. I5

explorer (ik•splôr′ər) A person who goes to find out about a place. p. 78

export (eks′pôrt) To send goods to other countries to sell. p. 136

F

fall line (fôl līn) The place where a river drops from higher to lower ground. p. 109

fictional (fik′shən•al) Describing a plot, setting, or character that is made up. p. 207

folktale (fôk tāl) A story passed from one generation to the next. p. 202

freedom (frē′dəm) The right of people to make their own choices. p. 84

free enterprise (frē en′tər•prīz) An economic system in which people are free to start and run their own business. p. 147

G

generation (jen•ə•rā′shən) A group of people of about the same age. p. 68

geographic tools (jē•ə•gra′fik tōōls) Tools that tell where a place is and what it looks like. p. 93

geography (jē•ä′grə•fē) The study of Earth's surface and the ways people use it. p. I2

globe (glōb) A model of Earth. p. I4

good (gŏŏd) A thing that can be bought or sold. p. 44

government (guv′ərn•mənt) A group of people that makes the laws for a community. p. 12

government service (guv′ərn•mənt sûr′vəs) A service that the government provides for everyone in its area. p. 21

governor (guv′ər•nər) The elected leader of a state's government. p. 24

grid system (grid sis′təm) A set of lines the same distance apart that cross each other to form boxes. p. 102

H

hemisphere (hem′ə•sfir) Half of the globe when it is divided into either northern and southern halves or eastern and western halves. p. I5

hero (hir′ō) A person who does something brave or important and sets an example for others. p. 195

holiday (hä′lə•dā) A day set aside for remembering a person, an idea, or an event. p. 29

human feature (hyōō′mən fē′chər) Something that people add to a landscape. p. 118

human resource (hyōō′mən rē′sôr•sə) A worker who produces goods and services. p. 130

I

immigrant (im′ə•grənt) A person who comes to live in a country from somewhere else in the world. p. 80

import (im′pôrt) To bring in goods from other countries to sell. p. 136

inset map (in′set map) A smaller map within a larger map. p. I6

interdependence (in•tər•di•pen′dəns) The reliance of producers and consumers on each other for goods and resources they need. p. 133

intermediate directions (in•tər•mē′dē•ət di•rek′shənz) The directions between cardinal directions that give more exact information about location, such as *northeast, southeast, northwest,* and *southwest.* p. I7

international trade (in•tər•nash′nəl trād) The buying and selling between countries. p. 136

Internet (in′tər•net) A system that links computers around the world. p. 169

GLOSSARY

interstate trade (in′tər•stāt trād) The buying and selling between states. p. 134

invention (in•ven′shən) Something that is made for the first time. p. 167

inventor (in•ven′tər) A person who produces something for the first time. p. 167

irrigation (ir•ə•gā′shən) The moving of water to dry areas. p. 116

J

jury (jûr′ē) A group of citizens that decides whether a person has broken the law. p. 15

L

landform (land′fôrm) A physical feature, such as a mountain, valley, plain, or hill. p. 106

latitude (la′tə•tōōd) Lines that run east and west around a globe. p. 103

legend (le′jənd) A made-up story about a real person or event. p. 204

locator (lō′kā•ter) A small map or picture of a globe that shows where the area on the main map is found in a state, on a continent, or in the world. p. I6

longitude (län′jə•tōōd) Lines that run north and south on a globe, from pole to pole. p. 103

M

manufacture (man•yə•fak′chər) To make goods by hand or by machine. p. 145

map key (map kē) A box on a map in which symbols used on the map are explained; also called a map legend. p. I6

map scale (map skāl) A part of a map that compares a distance on the map to a distance in the real world. p. I6

map title (map tī′təl) A title that tells what a map is about. p. I6

mass production (mas prə•duk′shən) The making of goods in large amounts by machine. p. 154

modern (mäd′ərn) Having to do with the time we live in today. p. 186

modify (mäd′ə•fī) To change. p. 113

N

natural resource (na′chə•rəl rē′sôrs) Something from nature that people can use, such as trees, water, or soil. p. 116

nonrenewable (nän•ri•nōō′ə•bəl) Not able to be made again quickly by nature or people. p. 129

P

physical environment (fi′zi•kəl in•vī′rən•mənt) The physical features of a place. p. 105

physical feature (fi′zi•kəl fē′chər) A feature of a place such as its land, water, or plant life. p. 94

pioneer (pī•ə•nir′) A person who settles a new land. p. 52

prime meridian (prīm mə•rid′ē•ən) The line from which longitude is measured. p. 103

production (prə•duk′shən) The process of making goods and services. p. 149

public servant (pub′lik sûr′vənt) A person who makes decisions and takes action for the community. p. 18

public transportation (pub′lik trans•pər•tā′shən) A method of moving large numbers of people from place to place. p. 179

R

raw material (rô mə•tir′ē•əl) A natural resource that can be used to make a good. p. 128

recycle (rē•sī′kəl) To reuse resources. p. 9

region (rē′jən) A large area with at least one feature that makes it different from other areas. p. 106

relative location (re′lə•tiv lō•kā′shən) The location of a place in relation to another place. p. 102

renewable (ri•nōō′ə•bəl) Able to be made or grown again by nature or by people. p. 129

representative (re•pri•zen′tə•tiv) A person chosen by a group of people to act or speak for them. p. 26

republic (ri•pub′lik) A type of government in which citizens vote for leaders to make decisions for them. p. 85

reservoir (re′zə•vwär) A human-made lake used for collecting and storing water. p. 118

revolution (re•və•lo͞o′shən) A fight for a change in government. p. 84

role (rōl) The part a person plays in a group or a community. p. 43

rural (rûr′əl) Having to do with the countryside, farms, and small towns. p. 58

scarcity (sker′sə•tē) A situation in which the supply of a product is not enough to meet the demand for it. p. 147

service (sûr′vəs) Work that a person does for someone else. p. 44

settlement (se′təl•mənt) A new community. p. 72

settler (set′lər) A person who comes to live in a new community. p. 74

society (sə•sī′ə•tē) A community of people joined together by similar ways of life. p. 46

specialization (spe•shə•lə•zā′shen) Doing one kind of work or selling one kind of good. p. 139

specialize (spe′shə•līz) To do just one kind of work or sell just one kind of product. p. 140

suburb (su•berb) A smaller community built near a large city. p. 57

suffrage (suf′rij) The right to vote. p. 81

supply (sə•plī′) The products and services that businesses offer consumers. p. 137

tall tale (tôl tāl) A story that uses humorous exaggeration to explain how something came to be. p. 202

technology (tek•nä′lə•jē) All of the tools that people use in everyday life. p. 167

trade (trād) To exchange one good or service for another. p. 133

transportation (trans•pər•tā′shən) The movement of people or goods. p. 119

tunnel (tun′əl) A path that runs through or under the land. p. 119

U

Underground Railroad (un′dər•ground rāl′rōd) A system of routes and safe houses used by enslaved people on their journey north to freedom. p. 197

urban (ûr′bən) Having to do with a city. p. 56

V

volunteer (vä•lən•tir′) A person who chooses to work without getting paid. p. 6

GLOSSARY

Index

The Index lets you know where information about important people, places, and events appears in the book. All key words, or entries, are listed in alphabetical order. For each entry, the page reference indicates where information about that entry can be found in the text. Page references for illustrations are set in italic type. An italic *m* indicates a map. Page references set in boldface type indicate the pages on which vocabulary terms are defined. Related entries are cross-referenced with *See* or *See also*. Guide words at the top of the pages help you identify which words appear on which page.

INDEX

INDEX

INDEX

INDEX

INDEX